DOCUMENTS OF MODERN HISTORY

General Editors:

A. G. Dickens
Director, Institute of Historical Research, University of London

Alun Davies
Professor of Modern History, University College, Swansea

THE GREAT POWERS
AND THE
NEAR EAST
1774-1923

edited by

M. S. Anderson

Reader in International History, London School of Economics

Edward Arnold

© M. S. Anderson, 1970

First published 1970 by
Edward Arnold (Publishers) Ltd.
41 Maddox Street, London W.1

Cloth edition ISBN: 0 7131 5553 1
Paper edition ISBN: 0 7131 5554 X

Printed in Great Britain by
Robert Cunningham and Sons Ltd., Alva

CONTENTS

VIII THE EASTERN QUESTION, 1878-1914

IX EUROPEAN ECONOMIC ACTIVITY IN THE OTTOMAN EMPIRE IN THE LATER NINETEENTH AND EARLY TWENTIETH CENTURIES

PREFACE

This is a small volume which attempts to cover a very large and complex subject. The problems of selection have therefore been considerable; and shortage of space has compelled me to jettison a good deal of material which I should have liked to include. In one respect at least I hope I may have been able to give a little breadth to the book; for since the diplomatic complications of the Eastern Question arose ultimately from the decline of the Ottoman Empire and the resulting weakness and instability of the Near East in this period, I have deliberately included a certain amount of material illustrating the weakness of that Empire and the struggles to reform it, as well as the later development of Turkish and Arab nationalism and the economic penetration of the area by the European powers. In other words I have tried to prevent the principle of selection becoming too narrowly diplomatic. In another way, however, I have deliberately restricted the scope of the book. Throughout the emphasis has been placed upon the major European powers, their relations with the Near East and with each other in the Near East. This means that, apart from a little material relating to Greece during the War of Independence, I have included virtually nothing on the development and policies of the smaller Balkan states. I regret this omission; but in view of the limited space at my disposal it seemed to me a logical one.

Where British Parliamentary Papers are quoted from the page numbers given are those printed within the paper from which the quotation is taken; they do not refer to the continuous pagination within each volume which was normally made in manuscript in the nineteenth century and by rubber-stamp in the twentieth. Dates are given in the New Style throughout.

M.S.A.

ACKNOWLEDGMENTS

The editor and publishers wish to thank the following for their permission to use copyright material: The *Archives du Ministère des Affaires Etrangères* (VII, 10); E. J. Brill (VII, 5); Cambridge University Press (IV, 5; III, 4); The Clarendon Press (VII, 8); Constable & Co. Ltd. (XI, 12); Walter de Gruyter & Co. (VI, 8); Harvard University Press (VII, 2, 4; VIII, 1, 11); the Controller of Her Majesty's Stationery Office (I, 1; IV, 2, 4, 5, 7, 8; VI, 1, 4, 7, 9, 10; VII, 11; VIII, 2, 3, 4, 7; IX, 2, 3 ; X, 3; XI, 2, 3, 4, 5, 8, 9, 11, 14); Österreichischer Bundesverlag (VIII, 13); Routledge & Kegan Paul and Macmillan (VIII, 8); the editors of *The Slavonic and East European Review* (VII, 3) and the University of California Press (X. 4).

ABBREVIATIONS

A. and P.	*Accounts and Papers*
B.D.	*British Documents on the Origins of the War, 1898-1914*, ed. G. P. Gooch and H. W. V. Temperley (London, 1926-38)
B.D.F.P.	*British Documents on Foreign Policy, 1919-1939* (London, 1947-)
B.F.S.P.	*British and Foreign State Papers* (London, 1825-)
G.P.	*Die grosse Politik der europäischen Kabinette* (Berlin, 1922-7)
K.A.	*Krasnyi Arkhiv* (Moscow, 1922-41)
Noradoungian	G. Noradoungian, *Receuil d'actes internationaux de l'empire Ottoman* (Paris, 1897-1903)
Pribram	A. F. Pribram, *The Secret Treaties of Austria-Hungary, 1879-1914* (Cambridge, Mass., 1920-1)
Temperley and Penson	H. W. V. Temperley and Lillian Penson, *Foundations of British Foreign Policy from Pitt (1792) to Salisbury (1902)* (Cambridge, 1938)
V.P.R.	*Vneshnaya Politika Rossii XIX i nachala XX veka* (Moscow, 1960-)
Zaionchkovskii	A. M. Zaionchkovskii, *Vostochnaya Voina 1853-1856gg.* (St. Petersburg, 1908)

INTRODUCTION

For a century and a half the Eastern Question was the most lasting and intractable of all sources of rivalry between the powers of Europe. The Russo-Turkish war of 1768-74 made clearly visible the extent to which the once-mighty Ottoman Empire had decayed and was now becoming the victim of more powerful neighbours. The Treaty of Lausanne of 1923 gave international recognition to a compact and relatively homogeneous Turkish national state. Between these two landmarks lay five generations or more during which the fate of the Ottoman territories, with all its implications for the prestige and the material interests of the great powers, was a central issue, or rather series of interrelated issues, in European international relations. To describe here, with any approach to completeness, the complex development of these issues during this long period, the twists and turns in great-power relationships which they involved, is impossible. All that can be attempted is to bring out some of the main forces which underlay these rivalries and to indicate some of the more durable elements in a fluid and complex situation.

The root of the matter was the inability of the Ottoman Empire to maintain the territorial position which it had achieved under the great Sultans of the fifteenth and sixteenth centuries. Its decline had been visible to acute observers, domestic and foreign, since the end of the sixteenth century. It had become more obvious since the later seventeenth century. But it was the defeats of 1768-74, and above all the severe terms which the Turks had to accept at the hands of Catherine II of Russia at Kutchuk-Kainardji (**I, 1**) which brought home to the statesmen of Europe how vulnerable the position of the Empire now was. Turkish weakness had deep social and intellectual roots: its ultimate causes lay above all in the stultifyingly conservative effect of still almost omnipotent Muslim tradition, in the power of the forces which for generations had opposed change of any kind. These forces, acting above all through the *ulema* and the janissaries, were able for long after 1774 to resist efforts at modernization and did not begin to be decisively weakened until the 1820s and 1830s (**V, 2, 3**). What, however, impressed European observers was not so much the real roots of

Turkish weakness as its symptoms, above all the growing naval and military weakness of the Ottoman Empire and the slowness with which these dangerous deficiencies were made good (**V, 1**). From the 1830s onwards there were endless promises and programmes of reform (**V, 3, 4**). Yet the evils seemed to grow, if anything, worse, at least in the eyes of European states, themselves rapidly developing and filled with a belief in the necessity and inevitability of progress. The years before the First World War saw criticism of Turkish rule (**VIII, 12**) at least as violent as any made a century earlier. What rescued the Turks from a humiliating and desperate position was not the preaching and exhortations of Europe but their own slowly-developing national feeling, seen in an embryonic form in the Young Turk revolution of 1908 (**X, 2**) and in a more conscious one in the National Pact of 1920 (**XI, 12**).

Throughout this period, then, the Ottoman Empire was slowly but apparently irresistibly contracting. More than once it seemed on the point of collapse – for example in 1839 under the threat of Mehemet Ali's armies (**IV, 5, 6**) or in 1895-6, with a pathological Sultan engaged in massacring a considerable number of his subjects (**VIII, 9, 10**). How were the territories it was slowly disgorging to be disposed of? What was to replace it, if and when it disappeared? Around these questions and the conflicting answers suggested to them the Eastern Question as a series of international problems developed.

In 1774 Russia emerged clearly as the main threat to the integrity and even the existence of the Empire; and this position she never afterwards lost for very long. The narrow foothold on the Black Sea which she had achieved at Kutchuk-Kainardji was decisively expanded with the annexation of the Crimea a decade later (**I, 2**) and further consolidated by the Treaty of Jassy of 1792 (**I, 3**). Simultaneously, and in some ways equally important, large advances were being made in the Caucasus. Some of the fears aroused in Europe by these Russian successes were exaggerated or at least premature; but the successes were none the less both brilliant and substantial.

The nineteenth century saw for Russia no territorial gains in the Near East comparable to those she had made under Catherine II. In part this was because of the slow improvement of the Turkish forces from the 1830s onwards, which allowed the Ottoman Empire on several occasions, notably in 1877 (**VII, 5**), to offer a stubborn resistance in face of Russian attack. To a large extent it was the result of the increasing support which the Turks were now receiving from the great powers, above all Britain, when threatened by Russian pressure. It was also, however, the outcome of the fact that Russian policy was no longer, as it had been, broadly speaking, in the later eighteenth century, one of unsophisticated territorial expansion. The desire for territory did not disappear, as witness the hopes of gaining much of Moldavia shown in the unsuccessful peace negotiations of 1811 and early 1812 (**II, 3**) and in the importance attached after 1856 to the recovery of southern Bessarabia which was eventually achieved in 1878 (**VI, 9; VII, 11**). Moreover the religious sympathies felt by so many Russians for the Orthodox populations under Turkish rule lost none of their strength and were supplemented from the 1860s onwards by the vague and enticing dreams of the Panslavs with their anti-Turkish and above all anti-German bias (**VII, 1**). But side by side with these territorial, religious and even racial ambitions went a growing realization that the continued existence of the Ottoman Empire, a weak neighbour which could not by itself be a threat to Russia and which might well play a valuable role in keeping the western powers out of the Black Sea and away from her southern frontiers, conferred important benefits on Russia (**II, 1**). This realization was given formal expression above all in 1829 (**III, 4**); and in 1833 Russia seemed for a time to have reduced her southern neighbour to the status of a satellite (**IV, 1, 2**). A desire to preserve Turkish territory intact as long as possible continued to dominate Russian policy in the Near East down to the Crimean War. Moreover, to the very moment of the collapse of the imperial régime in 1917, the Russian government, increasingly conscious of the grave weaknesses of the country when pitted against Britain or later Germany, continued to be very suspicious of any development which might weaken the Turks as an outer defence of Russia's southern frontiers (**VIII, 9, 10**). It is one of the great ironies of history that formal British and French consent to Russian physical control of the Straits and Constantinople was won only when the Russian Empire was approaching its death-agonies (**XI, 2**) and could thus never be exploited in practice.

In the later eighteenth century and during the Napoleonic period the main rival of Russia in the Near East was France. The invasion of Egypt in 1798, the most seminal event in the history of the modern Islamic world (**I, 4, 5**), was underlain not merely by the personal ambitions of Bonaparte and by a desire to strike at British power, but also by a long tradition of French political and commercial activity in the Ottoman Empire. The Russo-Turkish alliances of 1799 and 1805 (**II, 2**) were directed against France; and the conclusion of the Treaty of Bucharest in 1812 was forced on Russia by fear of French attack

(**II, 3**). As yet Britain's direct interests in the area were smaller than those of France: she was involved in it mainly from the standpoint of the struggle against the French Revolution and Napoleon (**I, 6**). By the 1830s, however, this position was clearly changing. By then Great Britain was becoming what she was to remain for half a century, the most consistent and effective adversary of Russian power in the Near East. The Treaty of Unkiar-Skelessi aroused in Britain much suspicion and even a sense of humiliation. Popular Russophobia was growing and in the hands of publicists such as David Urquhart (**VI, 6**) reached in 1853 a pitch at which it could exert some real influence on British policy. During the crisis of 1839-41, nevertheless, Russia was anxious to work in cooperation with Britain (**IV, 4**); and this helped Palmerston to take a strong and successful line in face of French partiality for Mehemet Ali (**IV, 6**). The outcome was a settlement which preserved the Ottoman Empire from what had seemed for a time a mortal threat posed by its Egyptian vassal and which for the first time created a régime of the Straits recognized by all the great powers as part of the public law of Europe (**IV, 7, 8**). Not until the Crimean War did Britain and Russia come to blows in the Near East.

During the earlier stages of the approach to that war it was still believed in St. Petersburg that Russia and Great Britain had important interests in common. In particular, the assumption that Britain was in the last analysis an ally against the newly-established régime of Napoleon III in France, and would cooperate with Russia if the Ottoman Empire collapsed, encouraged Nicholas I early in 1853 to embark on the ill-fated Seymour conversations (**VI, 4**). The events of the year which followed form the most striking series of diplomatic blunders and miscalculations in the history of modern Europe. On the Russian side the overbearing attitude taken towards the Turks in connection with the Menshikov mission (**VI, 3**), the occupation of the Danubian Principalities in July 1853 and the 'violent interpretation' of the Vienna Note of 1 August by which the powers had attempted to achieve a Russo-Turkish settlement (**VI, 7**), all seemed to show an aggressive and uncompromising temper. On the British side a desire to act in concert with France, and a deep-rooted fear and distrust of Russia which was now influencing not merely public opinion (**VI, 6**) but also many statesmen, allowed the country to drift into an unnecessary and unintended war. Moreover it was a war which settled nothing. The increasingly hostile attitude of Austria forced the Russian government to accept peace terms at the beginning of 1856 (**VI, 8**). But the Treaty of Paris (**VI, 9**), though it humiliated Russia, did little to weaken her: its most important provision, the demilitarization of the Black Sea, lasted for a mere fifteen years (**VI, 11**).

The Anglo-Russian rivalry in the Near East which had begun to emerge in the 1830s was further consolidated by the great Eastern Crisis of 1875-8. British distrust of Russian policies and ambitions had undoubtedly a certain element of the irrational about it, as Prince Gorchakov, for example, complained (**VII, 3**). But, brought to a head by fears for the safety of Constantinople and the Straits and of the possible consequences of Russian dominance of eastern Asia Minor (**VII, 7**), it meant that in the spring of 1878 the danger of an Anglo-Russian war had become for a time acute. Equally important and equally disastrous from the Russian point of view was the attitude of Austria-Hungary. Neither the unclear agreement made at Reichstadt in July 1876 (**VII, 2**) nor the military conventions signed early in the following year (**VII, 4**) could avert the emergence of Austro-Russian friction in the Balkans. Great Britain and Austria were united above all in opposition to the 'big Bulgaria' created by the Treaty of San Stefano (**VII, 6**); and within three months of the signature of that treaty it had been agreed that the newly-established autonomous principality should be drastically truncated (**VII, 8**). The Treaty of Berlin (**VII, 11**), therefore, though it brought Russia considerable territorial gains, was seen by many Russians as a defeat inflicted upon their country by Austria and above all Great Britain.

From the 1880s onwards the position changed fundamentally in a number of ways. The new power of the German Empire, in spite of Bismarck's reluctance to involve himself deeply in Near Eastern tensions (**VIII, 5**), was now playing willy-nilly an increasing role in the international relations of the area. The economic interests of the European powers in the Ottoman Empire were growing and changing their nature. The Suez Canal (**IX, 1, 2**) had almost from the moment of its opening become a supremely important artery of world trade. Later the Baghdad Railway (**IX, 3, 4**), far less significant economically, was to become a source of Russian and British uneasiness over possible German penetration of Anatolia and Mesopotamia. Above all the national feeling already rampant in the former Ottoman provinces in the Balkans was now spreading to the remaining territories of the Empire. Though Arab nationalism (**X, 1, 3, 4**) was still a minor force in 1914 it was also a growing one; and the Turkish revolution of 1908 (**X, 2**) was inspired largely by resentment of foreign interference in the Ottoman Empire. The rivalries of the powers in the Near East during the generation or more which followed the Berlin settlement were therefore played out against a background in which fundamental changes were taking place.

The Anglo-Russian rivalries which had been so acute and sometimes so dangerous for almost half a century still persisted during this period. Over the events of 1885-7 in Bulgaria (**VIII, 5-7**), as over the question of how Europe should react to the Armenian massacres in the middle 1890s (**VIII, 9**), Britain and Russia found themselves on different sides. But the tensions which had bulked so large in the age of Palmerston were taking a different form. From 1882 Britain, in possession of Cyprus since 1878 (**VII, 9**), was unintentionally and to some extent against her will established in Egypt (**VIII, 2-4**). Yet while her Near Eastern position was being strengthened, at least strategically, in this way, it was also being undermined, it seemed, by the growth from 1891 onwards of a new Franco-Russian alliance (**VIII, 8**). Moreover neither Salisbury nor any of his successors felt that keeping the Straits out of Russian hands was a really vital British interest. On the other hand Russia found that of her allies in the League of the Three Emperors (**VIII, 1**), Austria was definitely hostile to her ambitions in Bulgaria in the prolonged crisis of 1885-7 and Germany unwilling to give anything more than purely diplomatic support (**VIII, 5**), while her new French ally was in the 1890s most unwilling to underwrite extensive Russian ambitions in the Near East. The Austro-Russian agreement of 1897 (**VIII, 11**) therefore began a period of over a decade during which, in spite of continual minor upheaval in Macedonia (**VIII, 12**) there was no important Near Eastern collision between the great powers.

The Bosnian crisis of 1908-9 brought a new and acutely dangerous growth of tension. But by then the real power of Russia had been seriously reduced, at least for the time being, by the Russo-Japanese war and the revolution of 1905. Thus, when in 1908 Count Aehrenthal, intentionally or not, outwitted his Russian opposite number Izvolskii (**VIII, 13**) and annexed Bosnia-Herzegovina to the Habsburg Empire, the way was opened for perhaps the most humiliating defeat that the Russian Empire was ever to suffer in the Near East. The fact that it was German support for the Habsburg Empire (**VIII, 14**) which made ineffective the protests of Serbia, backed by Russia, underlined the leading role which Germany was now assuming in the affairs of the area. Her influence was emphasized still further by the Turco-German alliance concluded at the outbreak of war in 1914 (**XI, 1**) and by the influence over Turkish policy which she was able to exert until the collapse of 1918.

Two interlinked themes dominate the period of the First World War and the peace settlement – the efforts of the allies to agree on a partition of the apparently doomed Ottoman Empire, and the accelerating growth of Arab and Turkish nationalism. In a series of bargains sometimes arrived at only after hard and prolonged negotiation Britain, France, Russia and Italy agreed to take for themselves control of by far the greater part of Ottoman territory and to reduce what remained of the collapsing Empire to a pathetic rump in Asia Minor (**XI, 2, 3, 5**). Yet almost simultaneously the British and French governments, as a matter of expediency and without any sense of dishonesty, gave undertakings to Arab leaders which were impossible to reconcile with the terms of some of these bargains (**XI, 4**); and Great Britain, in the Balfour Declaration (**XI, 6**), made a promise to the Zionists which it was very hard to reconcile with those already made to the Arabs.

The result was that the end of the war made plainly visible in the Arab provinces freed from Turkish rule the hopeless contradictions which now existed between the aspirations of the politically conscious part of the population, encouraged by previous allied promises, and the realities of the situation (**XI, 9, 10**). The tangle of contradictory obligations in which Great Britain, above all, was enmeshed was all too clearly shown up. In spite, then, of the very considerable concessions made to Arab national demands in the Arabian peninsula, Mesopotamia and Egypt as part of the post-war settlement, it was obvious that the national grievances and ambitions which had now showed themselves would continue to afflict the area for a long time to come. In Anatolia the outcome of the war and the settlement which followed it was much more satisfactory. A long delay in imposing a peace-treaty on the Turks gave time for their national feeling, revived in militant form by Greek ambitions in Asia Minor, to become a dominant factor in the situation (**XI, 9, 12**). With the moral support of the new régime in Russia (**XI, 13**), and strengthened above all by the disunity and increasing weariness of the allies, Mustapha Kemal and his followers were able to make a dead letter of the harsh Treaty of Sèvres (**XI, 11**), belatedly imposed on the Sultan's government. The Treaty of Lausanne, a considerable though by no means complete success for the Kemalists (**XI, 14**), decisively halted the decline and contraction of the Ottoman Empire which had been in progress for centuries.

With the ending of that decline the root of the Eastern Question had been removed. The way was now open for the creation of the Turkish Republic as a stable and viable power of the second rank. Though the question of the Straits was still on occasion to engage the attention of statesmen this was no longer the burning issue it had sometimes appeared during the nineteenth century; moreover the war and the 1917 revolution in Russia had drastically and irreversibly reduced the importance of the Bosphorus and Dardanelles as a commercial artery. The problems posed by Arab nationalism were to become steadily more acute. But these were merely an aspect of the difficulties created all over the world from the later nineteenth century onwards by the spread of nationalist ideas from Europe to the colonial and semi-colonial areas she led and dominated. After Lausanne the Eastern Question as Palmerston, Nicholas I, or Bismarck had known it had ceased to exist, solved by events rather than by the wit or goodwill of man.

I

THE RISE OF RUSSIAN POWER AND THE FRENCH INVASION OF EGYPT

1 The Treaty of Kutchuk-Kainardji, 21 July 1774

This treaty can be seen as beginning the Eastern Question in its nineteenth-century form. Forced on the Porte by a Russian military advance deep into Bulgaria it persuaded many contemporaries that Russia was now a serious threat to the continued existence of the Ottoman Empire and therefore to the entire European balance of power. The treaty was particularly important as opening the way to future developments. Article III, which was bitterly resented by the Turks, laid the foundations for the Russian annexation of the Crimea less than a decade later (see **I, 2**), while Article VII was appealed to by the Russian government in support of the claims it put forward in its negotiations with the Porte in the spring of 1853. The provisions of Article XVI in favour of the Danubian Principalities provided a legal basis for a Russian interest in them which was to be reiterated in 1792 and 1829 (see **I, 3** and **III, 3** below).

Article III. All the Tartar peoples – those of the Crimea, of the Budjiac, of the Kuban, the Edissans, the Geambouiluks and Editschkuls – shall, without any exception, be acknowledged by the two Empires as free nations, and entirely independent of every foreign Power, governed by their own Sovereign, of the race of Genghis Khan, elected and raised to the throne by all the Tartar peoples; which Sovereign shall govern them according to their ancient laws and usages, being responsible to no foreign Power whatsoever; for which reason, neither the Court of Russia nor the Ottoman Porte shall interfere, under any pretext what-ever, with the election of the said Khan, or in the domestic, political, civil and internal affairs of the same; but, on the contrary, they shall acknowledge and consider the said Tartar nation, in its political and civil state, upon the same footing as the other Powers who are governed

by themselves, and are dependent upon God alone. As to the cere-
monies of religion, as the Tartars profess the same faith as the Mahome-
tans, they shall regulate themselves, with respect to His Highness, in
his capacity of Grand Caliph of Mahometanism, according to the
precepts prescribed to them by their law, without compromising,
nevertheless, the stability of their political and civil liberty. Russia
leaves to this Tartar nation, with the exception of the fortresses of
Kertsch and Jenicale (with their districts and ports, which Russia re-
tains for herself), all the towns, fortresses, dwellings, territories, and
ports which it has conquered in Crimea and in Kuban; the country
situated between the rivers Berda, Konskie, Vodi, and the Dnieper, as
well as all that situated as far as the frontier of Poland between the Boug
[sic] and the Dniester, excepting the fortress of Oczakow, with its
ancient territory, which shall belong, as heretofore, to the Sublime
Porte; and it promises to withdraw its troops from their possessions
immediately after the conclusion and exchange of the Treaty of Peace.
The Sublime Ottoman Porte engages, in like manner, on its part, to
abandon all right whatsoever which it might have over the fortresses,
towns, habitations etc., in Crimea, in Kuban, and in the island of
Taman; to maintain in those places no garrison nor other armed forces,
ceding these States to the Tartars in the same manner as the Court of
Russia has done, that is to say, in full power and in absolute and independent sovereignty. In like manner the Sublime Porte engages, in the
most solemn manner, and promises neither to introduce nor maintain,
in future, any garrison or armed forces whatsoever in the above-mentioned towns, fortresses, lands, and habitations, nor, in the interior of
these States, any intendant or military agent, of whatsoever denomination, but to leave all the Tartars in the same perfect liberty and independence in which the Empire of Russia leaves them. . . .

Article VII. The Sublime Porte promises to protect constantly the
Christian religion and its churches, and it also allows the Minister of
the Imperial Court of Russia to make, upon all occasions, representations, as well in favour of the new church at Constantinople, of which
mention will be made in Article XIV, as on behalf of its officiating
ministers, promising to take such representations into consideration,
as being made by a confidential functionary of a neighbouring and
sincerely friendly Power. . . .

Article XI. For the convenience and advantage of the two Empires,
there shall be a free and unimpeded navigation for the merchant-ships
belonging to the two Contracting Powers, in all the seas which wash

their shores; the Sublime Porte grants to Russian merchant-vessels, namely, such as are universally employed by the other Powers for commerce and in the ports, a free passage from the Black Sea into the White Sea[1]; and reciprocally from the White Sea into the Black Sea, as also the power of entering all the ports and harbours situated either on the sea-coasts, or in the passages and channels which join those seas. In like manner, the Sublime Porte allows Russian subjects to trade in its States by land as well as by water and upon the Danube in their ships, in conformity with what has been specified above in this Article, with all the same privileges and advantages as are enjoyed in its States by the most friendly nations, whom the Sublime Porte favours most in trade, such as the French and the English. . . . And in order to be consistent throughout, the Sublime Porte also allows the residence of Consuls and Vice-Consuls in every place where the Court of Russia may consider it expedient to establish them, and they shall be treated upon a perfect footing of equality with the Consuls of the other friendly Powers. It permits them to have interpreters called Baratli, that is, those who have patents, providing them with Imperial patents, and causing them to enjoy the same prerogatives as those in the service of the said French, English, and other nations.

Similarly, Russia permits the subjects of the Sublime Porte to trade in its dominions, by sea and by land, with the same prerogatives and advantages as are enjoyed by the most friendly nations, and upon paying the accustomed duties. . . .

Article XIII. The Sublime Porte promises to employ the sacred title of the Empress of all the Russias in all public acts and letters, as well as in all other cases, in the Turkish language, that is to say, 'Temamen Roussielerin Padischag'. . . .

Article XIV. After the manner of the other Powers, permission is given to the High Court of Russia, in addition to the chapel built in the Minister's residence, to erect in one of the quarters of Galata, in the street called Bey Oglu, a public church of the Greek ritual, which shall always be under the protection of the Ministers of that Empire, and secure from all coercion and outrage. . . .

Article XVI. The Empire of Russia restores to the Sublime Porte the whole of Bessarabia, with the cities of Ackermann, Kilija, Ismail, together with the towns and villages, and all contained in that Province; in like manner it restores to it the fortress of Bender. Similarly the

[1] The Mediterranean.

Empire of Russia restores to the Sublime Porte the two Principalities of Wallachia and Moldavia, together with all the fortresses, cities, towns, villages, and all which they contain, and the Sublime Porte receives them upon the following conditions, solemnly promising to keep them religiously:

1. To observe with respect to all the inhabitants of these Principalities, of whatever rank, dignity, state, calling, and extraction they may be, without the least exception, the absolute amnesty and eternal oblivion stipulated in Article I of the Treaty, in favour of all those who shall have actually committed any crime, or who shall be suspected of having had the intention of doing injury to the interests of the Sublime Porte, re-establishing them in their former dignities, ranks, and possessions, and restoring to them the property which they were in the enjoyment of previously to the present war.

2. To obstruct in no manner whatsoever the free exercise of the Christian religion, and to interpose no obstacle to the erection of new churches and to the repairing of the old ones, as has been done heretofore. . . .

7. Not to require from these people any contribution or payment for all the time of the duration of the war; and even, on account of the devastations to which they have been exposed, to relieve them from all taxes for the space of two years, reckoning from the day on which the present Treaty shall be exchanged. . . .

9. The Porte allows each of the Princes of these two States to have accredited to it a Chargé d'Affaires, selected from among the Christians of the Greek communion, who shall watch over the affairs of the said Principalities, be treated with kindness by the Porte, and who, notwithstanding the comparative want of importance, shall be considered as persons who enjoy the rights of nations, that is to say, who are protected from every kind of violence.

10. The Porte likewise permits that, according as the circumstances of these two Principalities may require, the Ministers of the Imperial Court of Russia resident at Constantinople may remonstrate in their favour; and promises to listen to them with all the attention which is due to friendly and respected Powers.

Article XVII. The Empire of Russia restores to the Sublime Porte all the islands of the Archipelago which are under its dependence; and the Sublime Porte, on its part, promises:

1. To observe religiously, with respect to the inhabitants of these islands, the conditions stipulated in Article I concerning the general amnesty and the eternal oblivion of all crimes whatsoever, committed or suspected to have been committed to the prejudice of the interests of the Sublime Porte.

2. That the Christian religion shall not be exposed to the least oppression any more than its churches, and that no obstacle shall be opposed to the erection or repair of them; and also that the officiating ministers shall neither be oppressed nor insulted.

3. That there shall not be exacted from these islands any payment of the annual taxes to which they were subjected, namely, since the time that they have been under the dependence of the Empire of Russia; and that, moreover, in consideration of the great losses which they have suffered during the war, they shall be exempt from any taxes for two years more, reckoning from the time of their restoration to the Sublime Porte.

4. To permit the families who might wish to quit their country, and establish themselves elsewhere, free egress with their property; and in order that such families may arrange their affairs with all due convenience, the term of one year is allowed them for this free emigration, reckoning from the day of the exchange of the present Treaty. . . .

Article XVIII. The Castle of Kinburn, situated at the mouth of the Dnieper, with a proportionate district along the left bank of the Dnieper, and the corner which forms the desert between the Bug and the Dnieper, remains under the full, perpetual, and incontestable dominion of the Empire of Russia.

Article XIX. The fortresses of Jenikale and Kertsch, situated in the peninsula of Crimea, with their ports and all therein contained, and moreover with their districts, commencing from the Black Sea, and following the ancient frontier of Kertsch as far as the place called Bugak, and from Bugak ascending in a direct line as far as the Sea of Azow, shall remain under the full, perpetual, and incontestable dominion of the Empire of Russia.

Article XX. The city of Azow, with its district, and the boundaries laid down in the Conventions made in 1700, that is to say in 1113, between the Governor Tolstoi and Hassan Bacha, Governor of Atschug, shall belong in perpetuity to the Empire of Russia.

Article XXI. The two Cabardes, namely, the Great and Little,[2] on account of their proximity to the Tartars, are more nearly connected with the Khans of Crimea; for which reason it must remain with the Khan of Crimea to consent, in concert with his Council and the ancients of the Tartar nation, to these countries becoming subject to the Imperial Court of Russia.

SEPARATE ARTICLE

By this separate article it is declared and established that the Sublime Ottoman Porte will pay to the Russian Empire in compensation for its war losses within three years and on three dates fifteen thousand purses, which is equivalent to seven million five hundred thousand piastres, and in Russian money makes up a sum of four million five hundred thousand roubles. The first date for payment shall be the first day of January of the year 1775, the second the first day of January of the year 1776, and the third the first day of January of the year 1777. On each of these dates 5,000 purses shall be paid by the Sublime Ottoman Porte to the Russian minister accredited to the said Sublime Porte.

. . . This separate article is to receive its ratification together with the whole of the treaty signed today, and we give it full force and effect as if it were inserted word for word in the above-mentioned treaty.

A. and P., 1854, lxxii [1735], pp. 39-47. The
text of the Separate Article is taken from
E. I. Druzhinina, *Kyuchuk-Kainardzhiiskii Mir*
1774 goda (Moscow, 1955) pp. 359-60.

2   The Russian Annexation of the Crimea, 1783-4

The independence of the Crimea decreed at Kutchuk-Kainardji (1 above) was always extremely precarious. The years after 1774 were a period of disorder and factional struggles in the khanate; and this instability involved a continual danger of a new Russo-Turkish conflict. By December 1782 Catherine II had decided to resolve the situation by annexation; the following extracts embody the rather artificial justification she put forward for this action and the agreement by which the Porte was forced to accept it.

(a) *Catherine II's Manifesto of 19 April 1783*

In the former war with the Ottoman Porte, when the strength and

---

[2] A large loosely-defined area east of the Sea of Azov, to the south and south-east of the port of Azov.

victories of our arms gave us every right to retain the Crimea, which was then in our hands, for our own advantage, we surrendered it and other extensive conquests for a renewal of good relations and friendship with the Ottoman Porte, having reorganized to that end the Tartar peoples on the basis of freedom and independence, so as to remove for ever occasions and means of conflict and coolness, which were often produced between Russia and the Porte when the Tartars were in their former state. . . .

But now, on the one hand we carefully considered the laying out up to now, for the Tartars and to their profit, of heavy expenses amounting at a true estimate to twelve million roubles, without including in this our losses in men, which are above all estimation in money terms; and on the other it became known to us that the Ottoman Porte was beginning to exercise sovereign power over the Tartar lands, and in particular over the island of Taman, where one of its officials, arriving with an armed force, publicly ordered to be beheaded the envoy sent to him by Shagin-Girei Khan[3] to enquire into the reason for his arrival and proclaimed the inhabitants of the area to be Turkish subjects. This act destroys our former mutual obligations regarding the liberty and independence of the Tartar peoples; it clearly proves that our proposal, when peace was concluded, that the Tartars should become independent, does not suffice to remove all causes of dispute between us, to strengthen the Tartars, and to ensure to us all the rights which were acquired by our victories in the former war and were established in full validity at the conclusion of peace; and therefore, because of our solicitude for the glory and greatness of the fatherland, endeavouring to safeguard its wellbeing and safety, equally deeming it a means of averting for ever the unpleasant incidents which disturb the perpetual peace settled between the Empire of all the Russias and the Ottoman Empire, which we sincerely wish to safeguard for ever, no less than for the compensation and satisfaction of our losses, we have decided to take under our power the peninsula of the Crimea, the island of Taman and the whole land of the Kuban.

> Khrestomatiya po istorii CCCP, ii, ed. S. S. Dmitriev and M. V. Nechkina, 3rd ed. (Moscow, 1953), 308

(b) *The Russo Turkish Convention of 8 January 1784*

Article I. The Peace Treaty of 1774, the Convention of 1775 relating to

---

[3] Ruler of the Crimea since the spring of 1777, but always unpopular with his subjects and regarded as a Russian puppet.

frontiers, the explanatory Convention of 1779 and the Treaty of Commerce of 1783 shall continue to be strictly and inviolably observed by both sides in all their points and articles, with the exception of Article III of the treaty of 1774 and Articles II, III and IV of the explanatory Convention of 1779, which articles shall no longer have any validity or binding force for the two Empires; but since in the above-mentioned Article III of the above-mentioned treaty of 1774 there is found the statement that the fortress of Otchakoff and its territory should belong, as formerly, to the Porte, this statement shall retain its validity and shall be observed as it stands. . . .

Article III. In taking as its frontier in the Kuban the Kuban river, the said Court of Russia gives up all the Tartar nations which are beyond the said river, that is to say, between the river Kuban and the Black Sea.

Noradounghian, i, 378

3   The Treaty of Jassy, 9 January 1792

This treaty ended the Russo-Turkish war which had broken out in August 1787. European complications made it difficult for Catherine II to exploit to the full the considerable military victories won by Russia; but by making the Dniester the frontier in Europe of the Russian and Ottoman Empires the treaty gave her the important fortress of Ochakov and once more strengthened her hold on the Black Sea. Notice also the continuing Russian interest in the Principalities (see Article XVI of 1 above) and the effort to defend the territories of the Georgian ruler King Irakli, who had accepted a Russian protectorate in August 1783, against raids by the Circassian tribes living south of the Kuban river.

Article III. In virtue of the second article of the preliminaries . . . the two high contracting parties have agreed by the present that for the future the Dniester shall for ever constitute the boundary of the two Empires, so that the territory situated on the right bank of that river shall be returned to the S[ublime] P[orte] and shall remain for ever and incontestably under its domination, as on the other hand all the territory situated on the left bank of the same river shall remain for ever and incontestably under Russian domination.

Article IV. As a result of the said clause relative to the frontiers of the two Empires ... H.M. the Empress restores to the S[ublime] P[orte] Bessarabia, as well as the towns of Bender, Akerman, Ismail, and all the towns and villages which that province contains.

Moreover, H.M. the Empress restores to the S[ublime] P[orte] the province of Moldavia with its towns and villages and all it contains, on the following conditions, which the S[ublime] P[orte] promises faithfully to fulfill:

1. To observe and execute religiously all that has been stipulated in favour of the two provinces of Moldavia and Wallachia in the Treaty of peace concluded on 21 July 1774, in the explanatory Convention concluded on 21 March 1779, and in the act of January 1784 which the grand Vizier signed in the name of the Porte.

2. Not to demand from these provinces any repayment of arrears of debt of whatever kind.

3. Not to demand from these countries, for the entire duration of the war, any contributions or payments; but on the contrary and in consideration of the damage and devastation which they have suffered during the said war, to exempt them for two years, from the date of the ratification of the present Treaty, from all charges and impositions whatever.

4. To allow families who wish to leave their country and settle elsewhere to depart freely and take with them their; goods and, so that they may have time to inform their relatives, subjects of the Ottoman Empire, to sell their movable or immovable property, according to the law of the land, to other subjects of the Ottoman Empire, and generally to put their affairs in order, they shall be granted a delay of fourteen months, to date from the day of the exchange of the ratifications of the present Treaty.

Article V. To prove the sincerity with which the two high contracting Powers desire, not merely for the present, to restore peace and good understanding between themselves, but also to strengthen it in future and avert all that may provide the slightest pretext for disputes, the S[ublime] P[orte] promises, in renewing the Firman which it has already despatched, severely to prohibit frontier commanders, the pasha of Akhaltzik or Akhiska, to disturb, from today, on any pretext whatever, secretly or publicly, the territories and inhabitants which are under the domination of the Khan of Tiflis, and to order them expressly not to interrupt relations of friendship and good neighbourliness.

Noradoungian, ii, 18-19

4 Decree of the Directory ordering General Bonaparte to launch the Egyptian Campaign, 12 April 1798

The attack on Egypt in 1798 was forced on the Directory, which would have preferred an attempt to invade England, by Bonaparte with the support of Talleyrand, the Foreign Minister. The stress in the decree on the need to strike at the alleged eastern sources of Britain's wealth should be noted, as should the assumption in Article V that the occupation of Egypt need not mean a breach with the Sultan.

The Executive Directory

Considering that the Beys who have seized the government of Egypt have established the most intimate ties with the English and have placed themselves under their absolute dependence; that in consequence they have engaged in the most open hostilities and most horrible cruelties against the French whom they vex, pillage and murder daily;

Considering that it is its duty to pursue the enemies of the Republic wherever they may be and in any place where they engage in hostile activities;

Considering, in addition, that the infamous treason with the help of which Britain became mistress of the Cape of Good Hope[4] has rendered access to India by the customary route very difficult to the vessels of the Republic, it is important to open to the Republican forces another route thither, to combat the satellites of the English Government and dry up the source of its corrupting riches;

Decrees as follows:

Article 1. The General-in-chief of the army of the East shall direct the land and sea forces whose command is entrusted to him to Egypt and shall take possession of that country.

Article 2. He shall drive the English from all their possessions in the Orient which he can reach and shall in particular destroy all their factories on the Red Sea.

Article 3. He shall have the Isthmus of Suez cut and shall take all necessary measures to ensure to the French Republic the free and exclusive possession of the Red Sea.

---

[4] The Cape had been occupied by British forces in 1795. The Statholder William V, who fled to Britain in January of that year, had ordered the Dutch authorities there to admit British forces for protection against French attack.

Article 4. He shall improve by all the means at his disposal the position of the natives of Egypt.

Article 5. He shall maintain, in so far as this depends on him, a good understanding with the Grand Seigneur and his immediate subjects.

Article 6. The present decree shall not be printed.

> *Correspondence de Napoleon Ier*, iv (Paris, 1860), 69-71

5 Bonaparte's Proclamation to the Egyptians, 2 July 1798

This proclamation, issued after Bonaparte's entry into Alexandria, illustrates his desire to respect Muslim religious practices and prejudices and to play down any idea of the French invasion as a conquest by Christians.

For long the beys governing Egypt have insulted the French nation and covered its merchants with exactions: the hour of their punishment has come.

For too long this assortment of slaves bought in Georgia and the Caucasus has tyrannized over the most beautiful part of the world; but God, on whom all depends, has decreed that their empire should end.

Peoples of Egypt, you will be told that I come to destroy your religion; do not believe it! Answer that I come to restore your rights to you, to punish the usurpers, and that I respect God, his Prophet and the Koran more than the Mamelukes do.

Tell them that all men are equal before God; wisdom, talent and virtue alone make them different from one another.

But what wisdom, what talent, what virtues distinguish the Mamelukes, that they should possess exclusively that which makes life pleasant and sweet?

Is there a good piece of land? It belongs to the Mamelukes. Is there a pretty slave, a fine horse, a beautiful house? They belong to the Mamelukes.

If Egypt is their farm, let them show the lease which God has granted them. But God is just and merciful to the people.

All Egyptians will be called to fill all positions; the wisest, the best educated, the most virtuous will govern, and the people will be happy.

Formerly there used to exist here, in your midst, great cities, great canals, a great trade. What has destroyed all this, if not Mameluke avarice, injustice and tyranny?

Qadis, shaykhs, imams, corbacis, tell the people that we are the friends of the true Mussulmans.

Was it not we who destroyed the Pope, who said that war should be waged against the Mussulmans? Was it not we who destroyed the Knights of Malta, because those madmen thought that God wanted them to wage war against the Mussulmans? Have we not been in all ages the friends of the Grand Seigneur (may God fulfil his wishes!) and the enemies of his enemies? Have not the Mamelukes, on the contrary, always revolted against the authority of the Grand Seigneur, whom they still ignore? They do nothing but satisfy their own whims.

Thrice happy are those who join us! They shall prosper in wealth and rank. Happy are those who remain neutral! They will have time to know us and they will come over to our side.

But misfortune, threefold misfortune, to those who arm themselves for the Mamelukes and fight against us! There shall be no hope for them; they shall perish.

Article I. All villages within a radius of three leagues from the places through which the army passes shall send a deputation to inform the general in command that they are obedient, and to notify him that they have hoisted the army flag; blue, white and red.

Article II. All villages which take up arms against the army shall be burnt down.

Article III. All villages which submit to the army shall display, together with the flag of the Grand Seigneur, our friend, that of the army.

Article IV. The shaykhs shall have seals placed on the possessions, houses [and] properties belonging to the Mamelukes, and shall see that nothing is stolen.

Article V. The shaykhs, the qadis and the imams shall continue to perform their functions. Each inhabitant shall remain at home, and prayers shall continue as usual. Every man shall thank God for the destruction of the Mamelukes and shall shout Glory to the Sultan! Glory to the French army, his friend! Curses on the Mamelukes, and happiness to the peoples of Egypt!

Correspondence de Napoleon Ier, iv (Paris, 1860), 269-72

6 The Anglo-Turkish Defensive Alliance, 5 January 1799.

By this treaty Great Britain acceded to a Russo-Turkish alliance signed two days earlier and helped to create, at least on paper, a very powerful anti-French coalition in the Levant and the eastern Mediterranean. The territorial guarantee in Article II constituted the most sweeping obligation ever undertaken by any British government in the Near East.

Article I. His Britannic Majesty, connected already with his Majesty the Emperor of Russia by the Ties of the strictest Alliance, accedes, by the present Treaty, to the Defensive Alliance which has just been concluded between his Majesty the Ottoman Emperor and the Emperor of Russia, as far as the Stipulations thereof are applicable to the local Circumstances of his Empire, and of that of the Sublime Porte: And his Majesty the Ottoman Emperor enters reciprocally by this Treaty into the same Engagements towards His Britannic Majesty, so that there shall exist for ever between the Three Empires, by virtue of the present Defensive Treaty, and of the Alliances and Treaties which already subsist, Peace, good Understanding, and perfect Friendship, as well by Sea as Land, so that for the future the Friends of One of the Parties shall be the Friends of the Two others; and the Enemies of One shall, in like Manner, be considered as such by the others. On this Account the Two High Contracting Parties promise and engage to come to a frank and mutual Understanding in all Affairs in which their reciprocal Safety and Tranquillity may be interested, and to adopt, by common Consent, the necessary Measures to oppose every Project hostile towards themselves, and to effectuate general Tranquillity.

Article II. In order to give to this Alliance a full and entire Effect, the Two High Contracting Parties mutually guarantee to each other their Possessions; His Britannic Majesty guarantees all the Possessions of the Ottoman Empire, without Exception, such as they stood immediately before the Invasion of the French in Egypt: and his Majesty the Ottoman Emperor guarantees all the Possessions of Great Britain, without any Exception whatever. . . .

Article V. Whenever the Two Contracting Parties make common Cause either with all their Forces, or with the Succours furnished by virtue of this Alliance, neither Party shall make either Peace, or a durable Truce, without comprising the other in it, and without stipulating for its Safety; and in Case of an Attack against One of the

Two Parties in hatred of the Stipulations of this Treaty, or of their faithful Execution, the other Party shall come to its Assistance in the Manner the most useful and the most conformable to the common Interest, according to the Exigency of the Case. . . .

Article X. In order to render more efficacious the Succour to be furnished on both Sides during the War, according to the Spirit of the present Treaty of Alliance, the Two High Contracting Parties will concert together upon the Operations most suitable to be made in order to render abortive the pernicious Designs of the Enemy in general, and especially in Egypt, and to destroy their Commerce in the Seas of the Levant, and in the Mediterranean; and for this Purpose his Majesty the Ottoman Emperor engages not only to shut his Ports, without Exception, against the Commerce of the Enemy, but likewise to employ against them in his Dominions . . . an Army, consisting at least of 100,000 Men, and even to augment it, in case of Need, to the Extent of his whole Forces: He shall also put his Naval Forces in a State of Preparation to act in concert with those of his Allies in the Seas abovementioned: And His Britannic Majesty, on His Part, reciprocally engages Himself to employ in the same Seas a Naval Force always equal to that of the Enemy, to annoy them; and to act in concert with the Fleets of His Allies, in order to impede the Execution of their Plans, and especially to prevent any Attack upon the Dominions or Provinces of the Ottoman Empire. . . .

Article XII. [The treaty is to last for a period of eight years.]

Journals of the House of Commons, lvii, Appendix (No. 11), p. 702

II

THE NAPOLEONIC WARS

1 Prince Czartoryski on Russian Policy towards the Ottoman Empire

Prince Adam Czartoryski, a member of a great and traditionally pro-Russian Polish noble family, had been one of the closest associates of Alexander I since the latter's accession to the Russian throne in March 1801, and became Deputy Minister for Foreign Affairs in January 1804. This memorandum expresses well the tension which was to exist for the next half-century between two different motives in Russia's Near Eastern policy— the desire to maintain the Ottoman Empire undivided as a weak and friendly state under strong Russian influence, and the desire for reasons of prestige and religious belief to aid the Orthodox Christians under Turkish rule.

Prince A. A. Czartoryski to Alexander I, 29 February 1804

There is no doubt that the Ottoman Empire threatens to collapse and that its future fate touches on the most essential interests of Russia. It is therefore urgent that our court should draw up a plan on this important subject in which every possible and probable case is foreseen, so that we can see clearly where we are going and proceed with assurance towards an immediate or eventual objective, according to the course taken by events. Our objective at the moment cannot be other than that of preserving the Ottoman Empire in its present state and hindering its partition. The advantage of having a weak and peaceful neighbour, and the facilities which our trade on the Black Sea has recently obtained, are sufficient reasons for contenting ourselves with the present state of affairs and preferring it to any opportunities which the future might offer and of which the consequences must always be to some extent uncertain. However I must point out that the facilities which the Black Sea trade has obtained, and which are for the Russian empire an object of the highest importance, result only from the extreme weakness of the Turkish government and from the quite unique circumstances produced by the war of the revolution. As a result, the facilities and the incalculable advantages in power and prosperity which may result from them must still be regarded as not entirely assured since we should lose them as soon as the Porte succeeded in regaining its former strength or if, intimidated by the threats of the French government, led astray by its cunning promises, it changed its policy and threw itself into the arms of France, or if finally any European power succeeded in taking possession of Greece, of its archipelago and soon afterwards of Constantinople. It is easy to see that, in this last case above all, the safety of the Russian Empire would be deeply compromised and one of the most essential outlets for her trade would find itself at the mercy of another power. Supposing that the Turkish government, forgetting its deep-rooted jealousy towards us and convinced of the danger it runs in lending itself to the projects of the French, should remain faithfully attached to Russia and unite sincerely with her if Bonaparte carries out his attack upon it, the safety and the fate of the Ottoman Empire will nevertheless remain very uncertain.

In proceeding in this important matter difficulties seem to arise at every step and we must, in a sense, navigate between reefs and take care not to run aground on them by taking the wrong course. The local circumstances of this country,[1] the links which the Russian court has contracted with the Turkish government and those which it cannot avoid having with the inhabitants whom that government oppresses and who oppose it, above all increase the difficulties; they are already embarrassing us in our present conduct and would become still more complicated should war break out in these countries.

Your Imperial Majesty, touched by the interest which you take in the conservation of the Porte, has been obliged to give orders for the reestablishment in the provinces under Ottoman domination of a system of surveillance and action which, if it ceased on our part, would allow the French to win an entire ascendancy over these peoples. Apart from this new factor, it is in the permanent interest of Russia, and in a sense a matter of honour, for her to maintain relations with the Greeks and other Ottoman subjects of the same religion, of whom she is reckoned the natural protector and who will always for preference be devoted to her as long as they can place their hopes in her. This policy has been followed by all the Russian sovereigns since Peter the Great, and to abandon it could not merely have results very harmful from the standpoint of our foreign relations but, I dare to say, would produce a bad effect even within Russia, since we should be abandoning a rule of

[1] i.e. the Ottoman Empire.

conduct not merely prescribed by the interests and dignity of the empire but also in a sense consecrated by the dominant religion of the country.

[If France attacks the Ottoman Empire Russia must support the Turks, but must also promise reforms to the Greek Christians and demand that these promises be honoured by the Porte.] It is difficult to foresee the events which might result from such a remarkable conflict of efforts, interests and different motives; but it is very possible, and this supposition must not be lost sight of, that matters may become so complicated and develop in such a way that they make the fall of the Turkish government and its retreat into Asia inevitable.

V.P.R., 1st series, i, 620–22

2   The Russo–Turkish Treaty of Alliance, 23 September 1805

This treaty was brought about largely by the increasing alarm with which the Russian government saw the apparently threatening increase of French influence and activity in the Balkans. The first secret article illustrates the continued predominance of Russia at Constantinople; and the whole document is in many ways a resurrection of the alliance made in 1799.

Article II. If any power should manifest views or intentions harmful to the two high contracting parties or to one of them, the other will employ its good offices to frustrate them. But if its intervention to smooth over the difference which has arisen and to ensure that it does not lead to a rupture should be ineffective, and if the efforts and resources of the party attacked should not be sufficient to ward off and repel the hostile enterprises with which it is threatened, then its ally shall be obliged to assist it with support in land and sea forces; but if in view of locality or distance it should not be possible for this help to be effective, then it shall be replaced by money in accordance with the valuation which will be made of the expense which effective help would have involved. If naval help is required, it shall consist at least of six ships of the line and four frigates, and if it is required in military forces it will be at least ten thousand infantry and two thousand cavalry: but payment in place of both military and naval support can take place only after a previous agreement to this effect. . . .

Article VI. If the efforts of the party attacked, supported by the auxiliary military or naval forces specified in the second article of this treaty or by both together, should not be sufficient to repel the attacks of the enemy, and if the auxiliary power should be in a position for its part to make war directly on the enemy of its ally, it will make it with all its forces and until peace has been concluded. But if because of the distances involved it should not be in a position to make war directly and to employ all its strength in it, and if the party attacked should desire that the number of auxiliary military or naval forces should be increased, in that case there will be an amicable agreement on the nature and extent of the additional aid which the party to which the request is made may add to that first provided. . . .

Article XI. [Great Britain and other states are invited to join the alliance.]

SECRET ARTICLES

Article I. . . . it has been reciprocally agreed that if, to hinder and destroy the projects of future aggrandizement of the French government, to bring about the reestablishment of the political balance and to procure the safety and tranquillity of all the States which the said government threatens, some of the great powers of Europe should decide to unite their efforts and to form a coalition, and that in that case His Imperial Majesty of all the Russias should decide for the good of his allies and all Europe to take an active part in such a coalition, defensive in its principles, the Sublime Porte . . . will make common cause with its august ally, the Emperor of all the Russias, or will at least provide to His Imperial Majesty the aid mentioned in the second article of the present treaty of defensive alliance and in a manner conforming to the stipulations of the present treaty. At the same time the Sublime Porte will take care to facilitate the passage through the Channel of Constantinople of the warships and military transports which His Majesty the Emperor needs to send into the Mediterranean during such a war, and it will conform to the salutary views of His said Majesty its ally. . . .

Article VII. The two contracting parties are agreed to consider the Black Sea as closed and not to allow there the appearance of any flag of war or armed ship of any [other] power whatever, and in case any power should attempt to appear there in arms, the two high contracting parties promise to regard such an attempt as a *casus foederis* and to oppose it with all their naval forces, as being the only way to ensure the tranquillity of them both.

3   Barclay de Tolly on the need for peace with Turkey

General M. B. Barclay de Tolly, War Minister when this memorandum was written, later commanded the Russian armies during the early stages of Napoleon's invasion of Russia. War between Russia and Turkey had broken out, largely as a result of increasing French influence in Constantinople, in December 1806. Barclay de Tolly's comments illustrate well the difficulties of Russia's position by the early months of 1812 as the danger of French attack grew, and the increasing pressure for peace with the Porte which resulted.

Barclay de Tolly to Alexander I, 3 February 1812

France, after subjecting to her yoke all Germany, establishing the Poles on our frontiers to do her bidding, hemming in everywhere and reducing to impotence Austria and Prussia, is in a position to employ massive forces against Russia, which may become even more dangerous if France finds a means of uniting her military forces in Dalmatia and Croatia with the Turkish armies. This will paralyse even our most happy successes on the Polish front, and will infallibly throw us back from the offensive to the defensive; and such a war can never end except unfortunately. . . .

The Emperor of France no doubt bases his hostile projects on the prolongation of this war against the Turks, and he fears peace between Russia and Turkey, since it will deprive him of one of the greatest weapons which he can employ against us. The Servians expect from this peace some improvement of their position, which will certainly be most unfortunate if this war continues and if, to concentrate our forces on our left flank, we are forced to evacuate all of Wallachia and abandon these poor allies to the cruel vengeance of the Turks. If unfortunately this catastrophe should take place, then all our influence is lost over the Greeks who, in spite of all the insinuations of other powers, still retain some attachment to Russia.

Peace with Turkey is surely the only means of avoiding war with France; for seeing us freed on our left flank and losing his influence over Turkey, Napoleon will not wish to expose himself to all the energy of the Russian nation, and to all the forces and resources so wisely deployed by Your Majesty on our frontiers. On the other hand if peace is not made he will be under an absolute necessity of making war on us even if he does not wish to, for having promised this to the Turks he absolutely must keep his word if he does not wish to lose for ever all influence in Turkey and make enemies there in place of friends.

Peace with Turkey is thus the first step which must be taken to make sure of success in a war against France. If this peace gives us the Sereth for our frontier it will be more advantageous for us than if it procured for us even the possession of Wallachia; for this possession will extend our military forces too far, and will always make Austria and Turkey uneasy, two powers which should in present circumstances be closely linked with Russia.

V.P.R., 1st series, vi, 267

4 The Treaty of Bucharest, 28 May 1812

This treaty ended the Russo-Turkish war on terms which, for the reasons indicated in Barclay de Tolly's memorandum of 3 February (**II, 3** above), were a good deal less favourable to Russia than had been hoped in St. Petersburg. Instead of the river Sereth and the Sulina mouth of the Danube, which they had demanded in previous negotiations, the Russians had to accept as the frontier the Pruth and the Kilia mouth, thus leaving the whole of the Danubian principalities under Turkish suzerainty. The reference in Article VIII is to the revolt (directed at first against the oppressive régime of the local Janissaries rather than against Turkish rule as such) which had broken out in Serbia in February 1804 and which enjoyed rather ineffective Russian support.

Article IV. By the first article of the preliminaries already signed, it is stipulated, that the river Pruth, from its entry into Moldavia to its junction with the Danube, and the left bank of the Danube, from this junction to the Kili [Kilia] mouth and the sea, shall form the frontier of the two Empires. This mouth shall be common to both. . . . As a result of the article mentioned below, the Sublime Ottoman Porte cedes and abandons to the Imperial Court of Russia the territories situated on the left bank of the Pruth, with the fortresses, towns, villages and habitations there, and the middle of the course of the Pruth will be the frontier between the two high Empires.

Article V. His Majesty the Emperor and Padishah of all the Russias returns and restores to the Sublime Ottoman Porte the Moldavian territory on the right bank of the river Pruth, as well as great and small Wallachia, with the fortresses, in the state in which they now are, the towns, cities, villages, habitations and all that these Provinces contain. . . .

The acts and stipulations relative to the privileges of Moldavia and Wallachia, which existed and were observed until this war, are confirmed, as has been stipulated in the fifth article of the preliminaries. . . .

Article VI. Independent of the Pruth frontier, those on the side of Asia and other places are reestablished entirely as they were formerly before the war, as is stipulated by the third article of the preliminaries. As a result the Imperial Court of Russia returns and restores to the Sublime Ottoman Porte, in the state in which they now are, the fortresses and castles situated beyond this frontier and conquered by Its arms, as well as the cities, towns, villages, habitations and all that this country contains.

Article VIII. In conformity with what is stipulated in the fourth article of the preliminaries, although it is certain that the Sublime Porte, following its principles, will show clemency and generosity to the Servian nation, which is, *ab antiquo*, subject and tributary to that power, however, in view of the share which the Servians have taken in the operations of this war, it has been thought suitable to make express stipulations for their safety. As a result, the Sublime Porte grants to the Servians a pardon and general amnesty, and they shall not be disquieted in any way for their past actions. [Serbian fortresses are to be surrendered to the Turks and garrisoned by them.] It [i.e. the Porte] will grant to the Servians, at their request, the same advantages which its subjects enjoy in the islands of the Archipelago and other lands, and will make them feel the effects of its high clemency, in abandoning to them the administration of their internal affairs, in fixing the amount of their tribute . . . and it will regulate all these matters in concert with the Servian nation.

V.P.R., 1st series, vi, 408-10

III

THE GREEK WAR OF
INDEPENDENCE

1 Declaration of Greek Independence issued at Epidauros, 27 January 1822

This declaration was drawn up by a congress of the leaders and representatives of the Greek rebels, and its emotional language and allegations of Turkish tyranny were well calculated to arouse sympathy over much of western Europe and in the United States. The appeal for unity in the last paragraph had no effect. There had been deep divisions from the very beginning of the revolt, notably between the relatively wealthy islands and the poor and isolated mainland areas; and by the end of 1823 factional rivalries had reached the pitch of civil war.

The Greek nation calls Heaven and Earth to witness that in spite of the frightful yoke of the Ottomans, which threatened it with destruction, it still exists. Pressed by the measures, equally unjust and destructive, which these ferocious tyrants, after violating their capitulations as well as all spirit of equity, made more and more oppressive, and which aimed at nothing less than the complete annihilation of the subject people, it has found itself absolutely compelled to have recourse to arms to protect its own safety. After repelling violence by the mere courage of its children, it declares today before God and man, by the organ of its legitimate representatives, meeting in its national congress convoked by the people, its political independence.

Descendants of a nation distinguished by its enlightenment and by its humane civilization, living in an age when this same civilization spreads its benefits in life-giving profusion over the other peoples of Europe and having continually before its eyes the spectacle of the happiness which these peoples enjoy beneath the protective shield of the law, could the Greeks remain longer in this state equally terrible and ignominious and see with apathy this happiness which they were conscious of, which nature has reserved equally for all men? Feelings so powerful and so justified could undoubtedly only hasten the moment of reawakening, when the nation, filled with memories and with indignation, must unite its strength to claim its rights and avenge for the fatherland a tyranny of unequalled horror.

Such are the causes of the war which we have been forced to undertake against the Turks. Far from being founded on demagogic or rebellious principles, far from being motivated by the selfish interests of a few individuals, this war is a national and holy one; it aims only at the restoration of the nation and its re-establishment in the rights of property, honour and life; rights which are the inheritance of our neighbours, the well-governed peoples, but which are torn from the Greeks by a despoiling power. . . .

Starting from these principles and sure of our rights, we wish for, we demand, only our re-establishment in the European association, where our religion, our customs and our position call on us to reunite ourselves to the great Christian family, and to take once more among the nations the rank which a usurping power has unjustly snatched from us. It is with this intention, equally pure and sincere, that we have undertaken this war, or rather that we have brought together the local wars which Mussulman tyranny set off in the different provinces and in our islands; and we march with a common accord to our deliverance with the firm resolution to obtain it or to bury our misfortunes for ever beneath a great ruin worthy of our origin which, amidst these misfortunes, merely weighs more heavily upon our hearts. . . .

Greeks, you have wished to shake off the yoke which weighed you down, and every day your tyrants disappear from amongst you. But only concord and obedience to the government can consolidate your independence. May the God of enlightenment endow with wisdom the governors and the governed, so that they may know their real interests and may cooperate, with a common accord, for the prosperity of the fatherland!

> G. F. von Martens, *Receuil de Traités*, xix
> (Göttingen, 1828), 144-7

2   The Anglo-Russian Protocol of 4 April 1826

This agreement was the product of an increasing willingness of Britain and Russia to cooperate in the solution of the Greek problem, a willingness which culminated in the sending of the Duke of Wellington on a special mission to

St. Petersburg in February 1826. It will be seen that Article III provided in effect that the agreement should not be dissolved by the outbreak of war between Russia and Turkey and left the door open for independent intervention by Russia. The terms of this protocol formed the basis for the Treaty of London signed by the British, French and Russian governments on 6 July 1827.

His Britannick Majesty having been requested by the Greeks to interpose his good offices, in order to obtain their reconciliation with the Ottoman Porte – having, in consequence, offered His Mediation to that Power, and being desirous of concerting the measures of his Government, upon this subject, with His Majesty the Emperor of all the Russias; and His Imperial Majesty, on the other hand, being equally animated by the desire of putting an end to the contest of which Greece and the Archipelago are the theatre, by an arrangement, which shall be consistent with the principles of religion, justice, and humanity;

The Undersigned have agreed:

I. That the arrangement to be proposed to the Porte, if that Government should accept the proffered Mediation, should have for its object, to place the Greeks towards the Ottoman Porte, in the relation hereafter mentioned:

Greece should be a dependency of that Empire, and the Greeks should pay to the Porte an annual tribute, the amount of which should be permanently fixed by common consent. They should be exclusively governed by Authorities to be chosen and named by themselves, but in the nomination of which Authorities the Porte should have a certain influence.

In this state, the Greeks should enjoy a complete liberty of conscience, entire freedom of commerce, and should, exclusively, conduct their own internal Government.

In order to effect a complete separation between Individuals of the two Nations, and to prevent the collisions which must be necessary consequences of a contest of such duration, the Greeks should purchase the property of Turks, whether situated on the Continent of Greece, or in the Islands. . . .

III. If the Mediation offered by His Britannick Majesty should not have been accepted by the Porte, and whatever may be the nature of the relations between His Imperial Majesty and the Turkish Government, His Britannick Majesty and His Imperial Majesty will still consider the terms of the arrangements specified in Article I of this Protocol, as the basis of any reconciliation to be effected by their intervention, whether in concert or separately, between the Porte and the

Greeks; and they will avail themselves of every favourable opportunity to exert their influence with both Parties, in order to effect this reconciliation on the above-mentioned basis.

IV. That His Britannic Majesty and His Imperial Majesty should reserve to themselves to adopt, hereafter, the measures necessary for the settlement of the details of the arrangement in question, as well as the limits of the Territory and the names of the Islands of the Archipelago to which it shall be applicable, and which it shall be proposed to the Porte to comprise under the denomination of Greece.

B.F.S.P., xiv (London, 1854), 629-32

3 The Treaty of Adrianople, 14 September 1829

This treaty ended the war between Russia and the Ottoman Empire which had broken out at the end of April 1828. It will be seen that Russia's territorial gains in Europe were small compared to those she made in Asia; but Articles V and VI, relating to the Principalities and Serbia, mark an important stage in the growth of Russian influence in the Balkans.

Article III. The Pruth shall continue to form the frontier of the two empires from the point where this river touches Moldavian territory to its confluence with the Danube. From there the line of the frontier shall follow the course of the Danube to the St. George mouth so that, leaving all the islands formed by the different arms of this river in Russian possession, the right bank shall remain, as in the past, to the Ottoman Empire. It is agreed, none the less, that this right bank, from the point where the St. George branch separates from the Sulina one, shall remain uninhabited for a distance of two hours from the river and that no establishment of any kind shall be set up there, and that the same shall apply in the islands remaining in the possession of Russia, with the exception of the quarantines which shall be established there, and it shall not be permitted to set up there any other establishment or fortification. ...

Article IV. Georgia, Imeretia, Mingrelia, Gouriel [Guria] and several other provinces of the Caucasus, having been united for long years and in perpetuity to the Empire of Russia, and this Empire having besides, by the treaty concluded with Persia at Turkmanchai on the 10th February 1828, acquired the Khanates of Erivan and Naktchivan, the two High Contracting Powers have recognised the need to establish between their respective territories, along all this line, a well defined frontier suitable to avert all future discussion. They have equally taken into consideration the means suited to oppose insurmountable obstacles to the incursions and brigandage which the frontier peoples have hitherto carried on and which have so often compromised the relations of friendship and good neighbourliness between the two Empires. As a result it has been agreed to recognize henceforth as the frontier between the states of the Imperial Court of Russia and those of the Sublime Ottoman Porte in Asia – the line which, following the present frontier of Gouriel from the Black Sea, reaches the frontier of Imeretia, and from there, in the shortest line, to the junction of the frontiers of the Pashaliks of Akhaltzik and Kars with that of Georgia, in this way leaving to the north and within this line the town of Akhaltzik and the fort of Akhalkhaliki at a distance of not less than two hours. All the territories south and west of this line of demarcation towards the Pashaliks of Kars and Trebizond, with the major part of the Pashalik of Akhaltzik, shall remain in perpetuity under the domination of the Sublime Porte, while those situated north and east of the said line, towards Georgia, Imeretia, and Gouriel, as well as all the littoral of the Black Sea from the mouth of the Kuban to the port of St. Nicholas inclusive, shall remain in perpetuity under the domination of the Empire of Russia. . . .

Article V. The Principalities of Moldavia and Wallachia having as the result of a Capitulation placed themselves under the suzerainty of the Sublime Porte, and Russia having guaranteed their prosperity, it is understood that they shall retain all the privileges and immunities which have been granted to them, either by their Capitulations, or by treaties concluded between the two empires, or by the Hattisherifs issued at various times. As a result, they shall enjoy the free exercise of their religion, complete security, an independent national administration, and full freedom of trade. The clauses additional to the previous stipulations, judged necessary to ensure to these two provinces the enjoyment of their rights, are consigned to the annexed Separate Act, which is and shall be considered as forming an integral part of the present treaty.

Article VI. The circumstances arising since the conclusion of the convention of Ackermann[1] not having allowed the Sublime Porte to occupy itself immediately with the execution of the clauses of the Separate Act relative to Serbia annexed to Article V of the said con-

---

[1] By this agreement with Russia, signed on 7 October 1826, the Turkish government agreed, *inter alia*, to reestablish all the privileges of the Danubian principalities and to grant similar ones to Serbia.

vention; it engages, in the most solemn manner, to fulfil them without the least delay and with the most scrupulous exactness and to proceed especially to the immediate restitution of the six districts detached from Serbia, so as to assure for ever the peace and well-being of this loyal and obedient nation. The firman, backed by a Hattisherif which shall order the execution of the said clauses, shall be delivered and officially communicated to the Imperial Court of Russia within a month, dating from the signature of the present treaty of peace.

Article VII. [Russian subjects are to have complete freedom of trade in the Ottoman Empire.]

The Sublime Porte undertakes, besides, to watch with care that the commerce and navigation of the Black Sea in particular shall not suffer hindrance of any kind. To this end it recognizes and declares passage through the Channel of Constantinople and the Strait of the Dardanelles entirely free and open to Russian ships under the merchant flag, loaded or in ballast, whether they come from the Black Sea to enter the Mediterranean or whether, coming from the Mediterranean, they wish to enter the Black Sea. . . . In virtue of the same principle, the passage through the Channel of Constantinople and the Strait of the Dardanelles is declared free and open to all merchant ships of powers which find themselves at peace with the Sublime Porte, whether they are going to Russian ports on the Black Sea or returning from them, loaded or in ballast, on the same conditions which are stipulated for ships under the Russian flag. . . .

Article IX. The prolongation of the war to which the present treaty of peace happily puts an end having occasioned for the Imperial Court of Russia considerable expenses, the Sublime Porte recognizes the need to offer her a suitable indemnity. This is why, independent of the cession of a small portion of territory in Asia, stipulated in Article IV, which the Court of Russia agrees to receive on account of the said indemnity, the Sublime Porte undertakes to pay it a sum of money of which the amount shall be fixed by mutual agreement.

B.F.S.P., xvi (London, 1832), 647-54

4   Report of the Special Committee on the Affairs of Turkey, 16 September 1829

This report of a special committee of six high-ranking officials, set up by Nicholas I under the chairmanship of Count V. P. Kochubei to consider the main lines of future Russian policy in the Near East, laid down a set of assumptions and principles which were to dominate the Russian attitude for nearly a quarter of a century.

The special Committee called by His Majesty the Emperor to give its opinion on the question of the affairs of Turkey having met, Count de Kotschoubey [Kochubei] announced briefly that the Committee would, in conformity with the intentions of His Imperial Majesty, occupy itself in discussing the political complications which the events of the present war might give rise to in the Ottoman Empire and which might result in its fall in Europe.

After this preamble the Committee heard the reading of a Memorandum presented by the Vice-Chancellor[2] and containing a summary of the principles and views which have guided the Russian Cabinet in the conduct of this war, as well as of explanations given at different times to the Allied Cabinets of the results which the war in the East might bring. In support of the ideas and reasoning contained in the Memorandum, there were read:

[Here follows a list of depatches, instructions and memoranda relating to Russian policy in the Near East in 1828-9.]

After having heard the reading of these various documents the Committee first of all thoroughly examined the situation of Russia in the grave circumstances of the moment and the course which her true interests command her to follow with regard to the Ottoman Empire. Impressed by the force and obviousness of the arguments developed in the documents submitted to the Committee by the Ministry of foreign affairs [sic], and struck above all by the justness of the considerations contained in the memorandum of privy [sic] Councillor Daschkoff [Dashkov]; in which the advantages and difficulties resulting for Russia from the neighbourhood of a state such as the Ottoman Empire are indicated and weighed against one another, the Committee unanimously recognized:

That the advantages of maintaining the Ottoman Empire in Europe are greater than the difficulties which it presents.

That its fall would henceforth be contrary to the true interests of Russia.

That as a result it would be prudent to seek to prevent it, by taking advantage of all opportunities which may still present themselves to conclude an honourable peace.

Starting from these principles, and before raising the hypothesis that,

---

[2] Karl Robert, Count von Nesselrode.

against the will of Russia and through the force of circumstances alone, the Empire of the Crescent may collapse in Europe, the Committee recognised that other situations might still present themselves; that the breaking-off of negotiations followed by the recommencement of hostilities would not necessarily lead to the fall of the Turkish Government, but that it was possible that the refusal of the Sultan to sign a peace treaty might lead to a new position, which, by allowing still to exist a last hope of prolonging the existence of this Government in Europe, must also be taken into consideration.

On this point the Committee has based itself upon the following suppositions:

1. That the Sultan would depart for Asia, at the moment when our troops were marching on Constantinople.

2. That a Revolution would break out in that Capital, following the approach of our troops, the consequences of which would be:

the raising to the throne of one of the sons of Sultan Mahmoud, and the establishment of a regency during his minority;

or a change of dynasty;

or an upheaval which would plunge the Capital and the entire Empire into confusion and anarchy.

The Committee after having carefully examined these different hypotheses, felt unanimously, that so long as a Mussulman Sovereign, with whom it would be possible to negotiate and make peace, still exists, the Commander in Chief should on no account reject an opportunity, which in any circumstances must be regarded as the most desirable and the most in conformity with the true interests of Russia; that therefore the departure of the Sultan for Asia would not decide irrevocably the fate of the Turkish Empire in Europe; that if in this perilous situation, he asked to renew negotiations and agreed immediately to accept our maximum terms, Count Diebitch should not refuse and should make peace with him; that if, on the other hand, the Sultan, while taking refuge in Asia, still persevered in his refusal, the consequence of his blind obstinacy would be for him, the loss of his possessions on this side of the Bosphorus and the Strait of the Dardanelles, and for us, the obligation to proceed at once to the carrying-out of provisional measures which will be indicated below.

If a revolution at Constantinople had for result, either the raising to the throne of one of the sons of the Sultan and the establishment of a regency, or a change of Dynasty, the Committee is of the opinion that neither of these events would be contrary to the interests of Russia, provided that it prolonged the existence of the Ottoman Empire, and that it might even become favourable to us, in placing on the throne a Sovereign less obstinate than Sultan Mahmoud, and less an enemy of the Russian Government; that as a result the new Sovereign, whether he were chosen from the sons of the present Sultan, or whether the choice fell upon a quite different individual whose selection offered us adequate guarantees, ought to be recognised and peace made with him, it being always understood in these different hypotheses that a peace can be signed without a loss of time equally damaging to our military operations and to the political calculations of the Imperial Cabinet. If on the other hand the revolution which broke out in Constantinople led to a general upheaval, the result of which was confusion and anarchy in the Capital as in the provinces, such an event could not be envisaged but as the signal for the fall of the Ottoman Empire.

In case therefore of this catastrophe, which we should be conscious of having sought to prevent by all the means in our power, taking place, as in that in which the Sultan, having taken refuge in Asia, continued to refuse our proposals and thus deprived himself of His States in Europe, it would become urgent to take certain provisional decisions on which the Committee has also been asked to deliberate. After examining those, which have already been prescribed by HIS MAJESTY THE EMPEROR to the Commander in Chief, as well as the measures proposed by the Ministry of foreign affairs, the Committee has agreed:

1. That Turkey in Europe would be occupied militarily by the Russian armies, until the fate of the countries which compose it should be definitively decided.

2. That this occupation should be made as imposing as possible.

3. That to this end Constantinople, the Castles of the Bosphorus and those of the Dardanelles shall have Russian garrisons.

4. That Widdin and some fortified points in Servia should be occupied by our troops.

5. That in no case should Belgrade be occupied by Russian troops, and that if the Turks were driven from it, this frontier fortress should be garrisoned by Servians.

6. That all other measures which the General in Chief may judge necessary to guarantee the safety of the army during the occupation, as well as the maintenance of public order, should be left to his prudence and solicitude. Complete latitude is granted him on this subject.

7. With relation to the diplomatic course to be followed, the Committee recognises:

That it would be contrary to all the rules of a sane policy to decide arbitrarily and without the agreement of the principal Powers the state of affairs which should replace the Ottoman Empire in Europe;

That it approves the ideas on this subject developed by the Ministry of foreign affairs, as well as the decisions which it has proposed;

That consequently a Declaration would be published by the Cabinet of Russia as soon as the catastrophe which threatens the Turkish government has been accomplished;

That this declaration would be conceived and drawn up in the sense indicated by the Vice-Chancellor.

Finally the Committee has resolved that, if the policies drawn up in the present protocol should be honoured with the approbation of HIS MAJESTY THE EMPEROR, Count Diebitch should receive a Copy of it, to serve him as instruction, which should be accompanied by the despatch of which the Vice-Chancellor has submitted the draft to the Committee.

> R. J. Kerner, 'Russia's New Policy in the Near East after the Peace of Adrianople', *Cambridge Historical Journal*, v, No. 3 (1937), 286-9

5   Convention signed by Great Britain, France, Russia and Bavaria, 7 May 1832

By this agreement the powers attempted to end confusion and disorder in Greece (where the murder of President John Capodistrias in October 1831 had been followed by civil war) by establishing the country as an independent state under the rule of a Bavarian king.

Article I. The courts of Great Britain, France, and Russia, duly authorized for this purpose by the Greek Nation, offer the hereditary Sovereignty of Greece to Prince Frederick Otho of Bavaria, second Son of His Majesty the King of Bavaria.

Article II. His Majesty the King of Bavaria, acting in the name of his said Son, a Minor, accepts, on his behalf, the hereditary sovereignty of Greece, on the conditions hereinafter settled.

Article III. The Prince Otho of Bavaria shall bear the Title of King of Greece.

Article IV. Greece, under the Sovereignty of Prince Otho of Bavaria and under the guarantee of the three Courts, shall form a Monarchical and Independent State according to the terms of the Protocol signed between the said Courts on the 3rd of February, 1830, and accepted both by Greece and by the Ottoman Porte.

Article V. The limits of the Greek State shall be such as shall be definitively settled by the negotiations which the Courts of Great Britain, France, and Russia have recently opened with the Ottoman Porte, in execution of the Protocol of 26 September, 1831. . . .

Article VIII. The Royal Crown and dignity shall be hereditary in Greece; and shall pass to the direct and lawful descendants and heirs of Prince Otho of Bavaria in order of primogeniture. . . .

Article X. During the minority of the Prince Otho of Bavaria, King of Greece, his rights of Sovereignty shall be exercised in their full extent, by a Regency composed of three Councillors who shall be appointed by His Majesty the King of Bavaria. . . .

Article XII. In execution of the Stipulations of the Protocol of the 20th of February 1830, His Majesty the Emperor of all the Russias engages to guarantee, and their Majesties the King of the United Kingdom of Great Britain and Ireland, and the King of the French, engage to recommend, the former to his Parliament, and the latter to his Chambers, to enable their Majesties to guarantee . . . a Loan to be contracted by the Prince Otho of Bavaria, as King of Greece.

B.F.S.P., xix (London, 1834), 35-8

IV

THE MEHEMET ALI CRISES, 1832-41

1 The Russians on the Bosphorus, 1833

Count A. F. Orlov, the author of this letter, was one of the most distinguished
and successful Russian diplomats of the nineteenth century as well as a trusted
agent and confidant of the Tsar. A Russian squadron, sent to protect the Sultan
Mahmud II against an apparently imminent threat from his powerful vassal,
Mehemet Ali, Pasha of Egypt, arrived in the Bosphorus on 20 February. It was
later considerably reinforced, while Russian troops were landed at Buyukdéré,
a few miles north of Constantinople, on 5 April. Orlov arrived in the Turkish
capital on 5 May, to combat British and above all French influence there, and
to sign if possible a defensive treaty with the Porte which would give Russia a
dominant position in the Ottoman Empire.

Count A. F. Orlov to Nicholas I, 25 May 1833

[A review of the Russian squadron in the Bosphorus by the Sultan
had been arranged for 20 May. It was raining heavily on that day and
Orlov suggested that the review be postponed.]

The Sultan, very conscious of this mark of deference, ordered it to be
replied that he did not wish to put off to another day a pleasure to
which he had been looking forward for so long. . . . The Sultan was in
a charming mood, and I may even say that he was touching in the
expressions of gratitude which he uttered for the generosity of Your
Majesty; he does not dissimulate his feelings and the sincerity of his
words is shown by his face. He stayed on the ship so long that finally
I did not know what to do about it; I was soaked to the skin. . . . The
whole diplomatic corps, and therefore the whole of Europe, was at the
windows of Buyukdéré and Therapia. Admiral Roussin[1] was seen with
an enormous telescope, which instead of helping him I think merely
impeded his view. . . .

We have only one regret here, and that is to leave without measur-
ing ourselves against the French fleet; apart from the complete cer-

---

[1] The French ambassador.

tainty that we should have beaten it, we are told on all sides that it is manned by youths who know nothing and that it is the laughing-stock even of merchant ships. You will understand, Sire, that this does not reduce our regrets.

Our relations with the Ottoman Porte are becoming more sincere, those with the Sultan no longer give rise to any doubt except for the feebleness of his decisions and his frequent lack of character. Roussin makes protests, but is always intriguing: the English are becoming more communicative, their connection with the French seems to be growing weaker.

T. Schiemann, Geschichte Russlands unter Nikolaus I (Berlin, 1904-19), iii, 432-3

2 The Treaty of Unkiar-Skelessi, 8 July 1833

This famous treaty, the greatest triumph of Orlov's career, did not in fact impose any new obligation on the Porte, since the closure of the Straits to foreign warships had been for centuries a traditional rule of the Ottoman Empire, relaxed only temporarily and in special circumstances. It had been explicitly recognized by the British government in 1809. However there were widespread though unfounded fears in Britain and France that the new agreement, while closing the Straits to the navies of other powers, gave that of Russia free passage through them; and it was undoubtedly intended by the Russian government to give Russia a special and dominant position in the Ottoman Empire.   •

Article 1. There shall be for ever peace, amity and alliance between His Majesty the Emperor of all the Russias and His Majesty the Emperor of the Ottomans, their empires and their subjects, as well by land as by sea. This alliance having solely for its object the common defence of their dominions against all attack, their Majesties engage to come to an unreserved understanding with each other upon all the matters which concern their respective tranquillity and safety, and to afford to each other mutually for this purpose substantial aid, and the most efficacious assistance.

Article 2. The Treaty of Peace concluded at Adrianople, on the 14th of September 1829, as well as all the other Treaties comprised therein, as also the Convention signed at St. Petersburg, on the 14th of April 1830, and the arrangement relating to Greece concluded at Constantinople, on the 9th and 21st July 1832, are fully confirmed by the present Treaty of Defensive Alliance, in the same manner as if the said transactions had been inserted in it word for word.

Article 3. In consequence of the principle of conservation and mutual defence, which is the basis of the present Treaty of Alliance, and by reason of a most sincere desire of securing the permanence, maintenance and entire independence of the Sublime Porte, his Majesty the Emperor of all the Russias, in the event of circumstances occurring which should again determine the Sublime Porte to call for the naval and military assistance of Russia ... engages to furnish, by land and by sea, as many troops and forces as the two high contracting parties may deem necessary. It is accordingly agreed, that in this case the land and sea forces, whose aid the Sublime Porte may call for, shall be held at its disposal.

Article 5. Although the two high contracting parties sincerely intend to maintain this engagement to the most distant period of time yet, as it is possible that in process of time circumstances may require that some changes should be made in this Treaty, it has been agreed to fix its duration at eight years from the day of the exchange of the Imperial Ratifications. The two parties, previously to the expiration of that term, will concert together, according to the state of affairs at that time, as to the renewal of the said Treaty. . . .

SEPARATE ARTICLE

In virtue of one of the clauses of the first Article of the Patent Treaty of Defensive Alliance concluded between the Imperial Court of Russia and the Sublime Porte, the two high contracting parties are bound to afford to each other mutually substantial aid, and the most efficacious assistance for the safety of their respective dominions. Nevertheless, as his Majesty the Emperor of all the Russias, wishing to spare the Sublime Ottoman Porte the expense and inconvenience which might be occasioned to it, by affording substantial aid, will not ask for that aid if circumstances should place the Sublime Porte under the obligation of furnishing it, the Sublime Ottoman Porte, in the place of the aid which it is bound to furnish in case of need, according to the principle of reciprocity of the Patent Treaty, shall confine its action in favour of the Imperial Court of Russia to closing the strait of the Dardanelles, that is to say, to not allowing any foreign vessels of war to enter therein under any pretext whatsoever.

The present Separate and Secret Article shall have the same forc and value as if it was inserted word for word in the Treaty of Alliance of this day.

A. and P., 1836, 1, 637-8

3 The Convention of Münchengrätz, 18 September 1833

This agreement, the product of a personal meeting between the Tsar Nicholas I and the Emperor Francis II, attempted to reestablish good relations between the two great conservative monarchies of Europe after the uneasiness which the apparent prospect of large-scale Russian expansion in the Near East had caused in Vienna earlier in the year. Widespread contemporary suspicions that a partition of the Ottoman Empire was discussed at the meeting were, as the text shows, unfounded.

Article I. The courts of Austria and Russia undertake mutually to implement the decision they have taken to maintain the existence of the Ottoman Empire under the present dynasty, and to devote to this end, in perfect accord, all the means of influence and action in their power.

Article II. In consequence, the two Imperial Courts undertake to oppose in common any combination threatening the independence of sovereign authority in Turkey, whether by the establishment of a provisional regency, or by a complete change of dynasty. If either of these situations should come about, the two High Contracting Parties will not only refuse to recognize such a state of affairs but will also consult immediately on the most effective measures to adopt in common, so as to ward off the dangers which such a change in the existence of the Ottoman Empire might entail for the safety and interests of their own States bordering on Turkey.

SEPARATE AND SECRET ARTICLES

Article I. The High Contracting Parties intend to apply specifically to the Pasha of Egypt the stipulations of Article II of today's public convention, and they undertake by common agreement expressly to prevent the authority of the Pasha of Egypt from extending, directly or indirectly, to the European provinces of the Ottoman Empire.

Article II. In signing today's public convention, the two Imperial Courts do not exclude from consideration the possibility that despite their wishes and joint efforts, the present order of things in Turkey may be overthrown; and it is their intention that if this happens it should not alter the principle of unity in Eastern affairs which today's public convention is designed to consecrate. It is understood therefore that, in such an eventuality, the two Imperial Courts will act only in concert and in a perfect spirit of solidarity in all that concerns the establishment of a new order of things, destined to replace that which now exists, and that they will take precautions in common that the change occurring in the internal situation of this Empire should not endanger either the safety of their own States and the rights assured them respectively by treaties, or the maintenance of the European balance.

The present separate and secret articles, having the same force and validity as today's public convention, shall be exchanged at Vienna at the same time as those of the afore-mentioned convention.

> F. F. Martens, *Receuil des traités et conventions conclus par la Russie avec les puissances étrangères,* iv (St. Petersburg, 1878), 445-9

4   Nesselrode on the Eastern Crisis, June 1839

This despatch of Nesselrode to the Russian ambassador in Paris shows clearly the desire of the Russian government, in the new crisis produced by Mahmud II's attack on Mehemet Ali in April 1839, to cooperate with the other powers of Europe, and above all with Great Britain. The danger of independent action by Russia of the kind taken in 1833 (see **IV, 1** above) was thus averted and the way opened for effective Anglo-Russian cooperation during the next two years.

Nesselrode to Count Pozzo di Borgo, 15 June 1839

The real danger for Europe at large is not in a combat carried on in Syria between the troops of the Sultan and those of the Pasha of Egypt.

Neither would there be danger to Europe if the Sultan succeeded in reconquering Syria, as he wishes and hopes to do. The danger would not begin to become serious until, in the event of the fate of arms declaring against the Sultan, the Pasha of Egypt should profit by this advantage to place the safety of Constantinople and the existence of the Ottoman Empire in peril. . . .

To prevent things reaching such a point, it is of consequence to take measures in time to confine the struggle between the Sultan and Mehmet Ali within certain limits, in order that this struggle may in no case extend itself so as to compromise the safety of the capital of the Ottoman Empire.

With this view, it has appeared to us essential to come to an understanding, frankly, with the Great Powers of Europe who, equally with
us, have at heart to prevent the danger which we have just pointed out.
Among those Powers Great Britain is incontestably the one that can
exercise the greatest influence over the fate of this question, and can
cooperate in the most decisive manner in realising the pacific intentions
of our august Msster.

A. and P., 1841, First Session, xxix Pt. I, pp.
96–7

5   Collective Note of the Powers to the Turkish Government, 27 July 1839

The defeat of the Turkish army by the Egyptians at Nizib on 24 June, the death
of Mahmud II six days later and the desertion of most of the Turkish fleet to
Mehemet Ali, seemed to place in question the survival of the Ottoman Empire.
This important note presented to the Turkish government by the ambassadors
of Great Britain, France, Russia, Austria and Prussia, was the product of the
alarm felt by the powers at the turn events had taken. It ensured that the Porte
would not surrender to the Pasha of Egypt and thus gained time for a settlement of the crisis to be attempted by diplomatic means.

The undersigned have received this morning, from their respective
Governments, instructions in virtue whereof they have the honour to
inform the Sublime Porte that agreement among the Five Great
Powers on the Question of the East is secured, and to invite it to
suspend any definitive resolution without their concurrence, waiting
for the effect of the interest which those Powers feel for it.

A. and P., 1841, First Session, xxix Pt. I, pp.
293–4

6   Palmerston on the Eastern Crisis, November– December 1839

These extracts from Palmerston's despatches are a good example of his tren-
chant style. They also show well the tenacity with which he struggled in 1839-
40 against French unwillingness to take effective action against Mehemet Ali
and against the widespread belief in Paris that the Pasha was too strong to be

evicted from the Turkish territory which he had seized. His insistence upon an international solution of the crisis, and in particular his willingness to cooperate to this end with Russia, should also be noted. Earl Granville and Viscount Ponsonby were the British ambassadors in Paris and Constantinople respectively.

(a) *Palmerston to Earl Granville, 22 November 1839*

With reference to Your Excellency's Despatch of the 18th Instant, marked 'Secret and Confidential', reporting a Conversation which Your Excellency had held with The King of the French, on the subject of the Turkish and Egyptian Question, I have to observe to Your Excellency, that the upshot of the remarks of His Majesty upon that occasion appears to be, that in proportion as the course of events have [*sic*] rendered the active assistance of the Powers of Europe necessary for maintaining the Integrity and Independence of the Turkish Empire, exactly in that proportion and precisely for that reason, the French Government has become unwilling to afford to the Sultan any assistance at all.

With respect to the notion that the Five Powers acting in union with the Sultan have not the means of compelling the Pasha of Egypt to evacuate Syria, that opinion is one which it can scarcely be worth while seriously to argue; the disparity of Forces between the two Parties in such a contest, being so infinitely great, that resistance on the part of the Pasha must necessarily be vain.

The King of the French, however, seems to be of opinion, that the Sultan would be more seriously injured in his Independence by receiving Assistance from Russia, than by having his Empire practically dismembered, and by being deprived permanently of the resources of a large portion of his own Territories. In this opinion, Her Majesty's Government cannot concur. It is undoubtedly a misfortune for a Sovereign to be under the necessity of receiving Military or Naval Aid from another Sovereign to defend him against hostile attack. The receiving of such Aid is a publick and undeniable proof of great weakness on the part of him who receives it; and real Independence is not compatible with great weakness. Such aid also, if given by the single Act of the Sovereign who affords it, entitles that Sovereign to ask in return favours and influence, which must trench upon the future Independence of the Sovereign who has been protected. But if Russia were to give Assistance to the Sultan, not as acting upon her own single Decision, but as acting in pursuance of a Concert between the Five Allied Powers, such Assistance would of course not bring after it any favours or concessions from Turkey to Russia; and then, the only question would be, whether the Independence of the Turkish Empire would permanently and for the future, be most affected, by the temporary occupation of some part of the Turkish Territory by a friendly Russian Force, which would come in to restore that Territory to the Sultan, and which would go out again, when that purpose was accomplished; or by the permanent occupation of such Territory by a hostile Egyptian Force, which having come in to conquer, would stay in to retain; and would by retaining, practically sever such Territory from the Turkish Empire. But surely there can be no doubt how that Question must be answered.

Public Record Office, F.O. 146/211; printed in Temperley and Penson, pp. 128-30

(b) *Palmerston to Viscount Ponsonby, 2 December 1839*

I have to instruct Your Excellency to continue to urge the Turkish Government to remain firm, to make no concession to Mehemet Ali, but to trust to the support of its Allies. The British Government has taken its line; and the course of the negotiations during the last few Months ought to inspire the Turkish Government with confidence in Great Britain. For it has been the British Government which has mainly prevented the Porte from being pressed by the Five Powers to submit unconditionally to all the demands of Mehemet Ali. France has for some time declared her opinion, that such a settlement is the only one that is practicable; and she has laboured to persuade the other Powers to adopt her views. If Great Britain had given way to France, and had consented to support the French propositions, Austria, and Prussia, and Russia would probably have acquiesced in them also: because those Powers have intimated that they would support any arrangement which England and France should have agreed upon. But England has stood firm to the Principles which she laid down in the outset of the negotiation, and her steadiness has encouraged Austria to adhere to the same line, while it has made it impossible for Russia to adopt the views of France, even if she had been disposed to do so; because Russia, having contracted special engagements to protect Turkey, could not appear to be less friendly to that Power than England is. In like manner the avowed desire of France to support the pretensions of Mehemet Ali has led to no result, and will lead to none as long as the Porte is true to its own Interests.

Public Record Office, F.O. 195/158; printed in Temperley and Penson, pp. 127-8

7 Convention for the Pacification of the Levant, 15 July 1840

The signature of this convention by Great Britain, Russia, Austria and Prussia meant that the efforts to find a settlement of the eastern crisis acceptable to France, which had taken up much time and energy in the past eight or nine months, had been abandoned. The signatories agreed that its terms should not be disclosed to the French government. The relatively generous offer made to Mehemet Ali reflects the continuing respect felt for his military strength (though this was soon to be undermined by the successful rising against Egyptian rule which broke out in the Lebanon in September) and still more the unwillingness of the powers, and in particular of Palmerston, to push matters to a conclusion against him. The 'rule of the Straits' laid down in Article IV was to be reiterated in the Straits Convention of July 1841 (see **IV, 8** below).

CONVENTION

Article I. His Highness the Sultan having come to an agreement with their Majesties the Queen of the United Kingdom of Great Britain and Ireland, the Emperor of Austria, King of Hungary and Bohemia, the King of Prussia, and the Emperor of all the Russias, as to the conditions of the arrangement which it is the intention of His Highness to grant to Mehemet Ali, conditions which are specified in the Separate Act hereunto annexed; Their Majesties engage to act in perfect accord, and to unite their efforts in order to determine Mehemet Ali to conform to that arrangement; each of the High Contracting Parties reserving to itself to cooperate for that purpose, according to the means of action which each may have at its disposal.

Article II. If the Pasha of Egypt should refuse to accept the above-mentioned arrangement, which will be communicated to him by the Sultan, with the concurrence of Their aforesaid Majesties; Their Majesties engage to take, at the request of the Sultan, measures concerted and settled between Them, in order to carry that arrangement into effect. . . . [In the meanwhile the British and Austrian governments will give orders to their Mediterranean squadrons to intercept the communications between Egypt and Syria by sea.]

Article III. If Mehemet Ali, after having refused to submit to the conditions of the arrangement above-mentioned, should direct his land or sea forces against Constantinople, the High Contracting Parties, upon the express demand of the Sultan, addressed to their representatives at Constantinople, agree, in such case, to comply with the request of that Sovereign, and to provide for the defence of his throne by means of a cooperation agreed upon by mutual consent, for the purpose of placing the two Straits of the Bosphorus and Dardanelles, as well as the Capital of the Ottoman Empire, in security against all aggression. . . . [Forces so engaged are to withdraw simultaneously when the Sultan considers their presence no longer necessary.]

Article IV. It is, however, expressly understood, that the cooperation mentioned in the preceding Article, and destined to place the Straits of the Dardanelles and of the Bosphorus, and the Ottoman Capital, under the temporary safeguard of the High Contracting Parties against all aggression of Mehemet Ali, shall be considered only as a measure of exception adopted at the express demand of the Sultan, and solely for his defence in the single case above-mentioned; but it is agreed, that such measure shall not derogate in any degree from the ancient rule of the Ottoman Empire, in virtue of which it has at all times been prohibited for ships of war of Foreign Powers to enter the Straits of the Dardanelles and of the Bosphorus. And the Sultan, on the one hand, hereby declares that, excepting the contingency above-mentioned, it is his firm resolution to maintain in future this principle invariably established as the ancient rule of his Empire; and as long as the Porte is at peace, to admit no foreign ship of war into the Straits of the Bosphorus and of the Dardanelles; on the other hand, their Majesties the Queen of the United Kingdom of Great Britain and Ireland, the Emperor of Austria, King of Hungary and Bohemia, the King of Prussia, and the Emperor of all the Russias, engage to respect this determination of the Sultan, and to conform to the above-mentioned principle.

SEPARATE ACT

Article 1. His Highness promises to grant to Mehemet Ali, for himself and for his descendants in the direct line, the administration of the Pashalic of Egypt; and His Highness promises, moreover, to grant to Mehemet Ali, for his life, with the title of Pasha of Acre, and with the command of the Fortress of St. John of Acre, the administration of the southern part of Syria, the limits of which shall be determined by the following line of demarkation: . . . [Details follow.]

The Sultan, however, in making these offers, attaches thereto the condition, that Mehemet Ali shall accept them within the space of ten days after communication thereof shall have been made to him at Alexandria, by an agent of His Highness; and that Mehemet Ali shall, at the same time, place in the hands of that agent the necessary instructions to the Commanders of his sea and land forces, to withdraw immediately from Arabia, and from all the Holy Cities which are therein situated; from the Island of Candia; from the district of Adana; and from all other parts of the Ottoman Empire which are not comprised within the limits of Egypt, and within those of the Pashalic of Acre, as above defined.

Article 2. If within the space of ten days, fixed as above, Mehemet Ali should not accept the above-mentioned arrangement, the Sultan will then withdraw the offer of the life administration of the Pashalic of Acre; but His Highness will still consent to grant to Mehemet Ali, for himself and for his descendants in the direct line, the administration of the Pashalic of Egypt, provided such offer be accepted within the space of the ten days next following; that is to say, within a period of twenty days, to be reckoned from the day on which the communication shall have been made to him. . . .

Article 7. If, at the expiration of the period of twenty days after the communication shall have been made to him (according to the stipulation of Article 2), Mehemet Ali shall not accede to the proposed arrangement, and shall not accept the hereditary Pashalic of Egypt, the Sultan will consider himself at liberty to withdraw that offer, and to follow, in consequence, such ulterior course as his own interests, and the counsels of his Allies, may suggest to him.

A. and P., 1841, First Session, xxix Pt. I,
pp. 691-3, 696-7

8   The Straits Convention, 13 July 1841

This agreement, of which France, now reconciled to the other great powers, was a signatory, reiterated and emphasized the provision regarding the Straits of the four-power convention of 15 July 1840 (see **IV, 7** above). The 'régime of the Straits' which it established was to be an important element in the international law of Europe until the First World War, though its exact significance could still be disputed.

Their Majesties the Emperor of Austria, King of Hungary and Bohemia, the King of the French, the Queen of the United Kingdom of Great Britain and Ireland, the King of Prussia, and the Emperor of all the Russias, being persuaded that their union and their agreement offer to Europe the most certain pledge for the preservation of the general peace, the constant object of their solicitude; and their said Majesties being desirous of testifying this agreement by giving to the Sultan a manifest proof of the respect which they entertain for the inviolability of his sovereign rights, as well as of their sincere desire to see consolidated the repose of his empire; their said Majesties have resolved to comply with the invitation of His Highness the Sultan, in order to record in common, by a formal Act, their unanimous determination to conform to the ancient rule of the Ottoman Empire, according to which the passage of the Straits of the Dardanelles and of the Bosphorus is always to be closed to foreign ships of war, so long as the Porte is at peace. . . .

Article I. His Highness the Sultan, on the one part, declares that he is firmly resolved to maintain for the future the principle invariably established as the ancient rule of his empire, and in virtue of which it has at all times been prohibited for the Ships of War of Foreign Powers to enter the Straits of the Dardanelles and of the Bosphorus; and that, so long as the Porte is at peace, His Highness will admit no foreign ship of war into the said Straits.

And their Majesties the Emperor of Austria, King of Hungary and Bohemia, the King of the French, the Queen of the United Kingdom of Great Britain and Ireland, the King of Prussia, and the Emperor of all the Russias, on the other part, engage to respect this determination of the Sultan and to conform themselves to the principle above specified.

Article II. It is understood that in recording the inviolability of the ancient rule of the Ottoman Empire mentioned in the preceding Article, the Sultan reserves to himself, as in past times, to deliver firmans of passage for light vessels under flag of war, which shall be employed as is usual in the service of the Missions of Foreign Powers.

Article III. His Highness the Sultan reserves to himself to communicate the present Convention to all the Powers with whom the Sublime Porte is in relations of friendship, inviting them to accede thereto.

                              A. and P., 1841, Second Session, viii Pt. III, 324

V

THE STRUGGLE FOR INTERNAL REFORM IN THE OTTOMAN EMPIRE

1 Thornton on the Naval and Military Weakness of the Ottoman Empire

Thomas Thornton was probably as well acquainted with the Ottoman Empire as any Englishman of his time. He was a merchant in Constantinople for fourteen years, during which time he travelled extensively in both European and Asiatic Turkey and lived for over a year in Odessa in south Russia. His criticisms of some aspects of Turkish life are given point by the fact that his general attitude in the book is very favourable to the Turks. These extracts illustrate the weaknesses of the Ottoman Empire which seemed to foreigners to call most urgently for reform in the later eighteenth and early nineteenth centuries.

I went on board some ships of war on their return from a cruise in the Black Sea, in the year 1790, and certainly saw a confusion which it is impossible to describe. It was a perfect *bazar*, or market-place, and shops were erected all round the between-decks, with no apparent intention of removing them. . . . Their navy now consists of several good ships, built by Europeans, or from European models, but manned by people unaccustomed to the sea. They have not yet formed any plan for educating and training up seamen, though the Propontis[1] is well adapted for naval evolutions, and might be made an excellent school of practical navigation. Their officers, not having passed through the different ranks, merit no higher estimation than the common men; indeed almost the whole business of the ship is performed by the slaves, or by the Greeks who are retained upon wages.

Those accustomed to the strict subordination and punctilious for-

[1] The Black Sea.

malities established in the armies and navies of other European powers, may smile perhaps at hearing, that the captain of a man of war has been cuffed in public by the admiral's own hand for a slight offence. I remember too to have seen a journal kept by an Englishman (an adventurer who served on board the Turkish fleet in the Black Sea, during a cruise in the year 1790) which contained the following remark. 'This day the admiral amused himself with playing at chess on the quarter-deck with a common sailor.' . . .

The force of the Turkish empire is a militia composed of the total mass of the Mussulman subjects; but uninformed, undisciplined, and intractable: if compared to a European army, they are merely a disorderly crowd. The finances, in the calculation of which violence and extortion always formed a principal part, are incapable of being improved, so as to be sufficient for the support of a regular standing army, by any constitutional means, or by any means which the people, instigated by turbulent and ambitious leaders, would not efficaciously oppose: so that, notwithstanding the efforts of the porte [sic] towards ameliorating their military system and introducing European improvements, there is little ground for expecting, that they will ever again bring their armies into the field, on this side of the Bosphorus, against a foreign enemy, unless impelled by despair or aided by a powerful ally. To oppose a rebel in a distant province, a neighbouring pasha must be stimulated by the allurement of conquest and plunder, or incited by rewards and the promise of new dignities. The governor of an insignificant fortress, at no very great distance from the capital, not long ago insulted the government, almost at the gates of the seraglio, and baffled the utmost efforts o the porte: the late capudan pasha, Hussein, was compelled to sacrifice his own honour, together with the dignity of the sultan, to the humiliation of treating with a revolted subject; and, at this time, there is no province in Romelia, where troops of licentious banditti do not annually intercept the caravans, interrupt communication, plunder the husbandman, and desolate the country.

T. Thornton, *The Present State of Turkey*, 2nd ed. (London, 1809), i, 293-5; ii, 64-6

2 Walsh describes the Massacre of the Janissaries, 1826

The last of many revolts of the janissaries was provoked, perhaps intentionally, by a decree of the reforming Sultan, Mahmud II, of 28 May. This called for the creation of a new military force, organized on modern lines, to which each janissary battalion in the capital was to contribute one hundred and fifty men. The ferocious suppression of the mutiny, here described, was followed by the abolition of the janissary corps, an essential step towards the modernization of the army and of government in general and therefore a turning-point in Turkish history. The author of this description was chaplain of the British embassy at Constantinople at the time of the massacre.

On the 13th of June they assembled as usual to practise their new exercise; one of the Egyptian officers, who had ten recruits to instruct, was vexed at the real or affected awkwardness of a surly fellow among them, and struck him a blow to correct his inattention. The fellow immediately appealed to his comrades, and so worked upon their excitable feelings, that they swore to destroy every person who had been instruments in introducing the new system. Sixty, therefore, of the most implacable and determined, secretly assembled on the night of the 14th of June, armed with pistols, topheks, and yatigans, and, headed by the man who had been struck, marched out at midnight, and proceeded to attack the palace of the Yenitchery Aghassi: they found the gates closed, but they soon burst them open, and then rushed in and sacrificed on the spot everyone they met with. They then demanded the chief of the Janissaries, Delhi Mehmet Aga, to cut him to pieces, as they openly declared was their intention. They were informed that he was in the harem with his females, a place hitherto held sacred by every Turk, however rude and brutal; but these men seemed now determined to hold nothing sacred; they burst open the doors of these hallowed chambers, and rushed in among the astonished and terrified women, who were suddenly roused from their beds, and ran about nearly in a state of nudity among those ferocious men. The chief was nowhere to be found; on the first alarm he had fled by a secret door and a ladder provided for such emergency, and so, by a few minutes, escaped the yatigans of the assassins. . . .

[They then plundered the palaces of several other dignitaries whom they regarded as their enemies, and the revolt became a general one of the whole janissary corps; while the troops who supported the Sultan were rapidly concentrated in large numbers.]

The janissaries, however, were now confident of success; the whole effective force had solemnly assembled round their inverted kettles, in the hallowed spot of the Etmeidan, from whence they had, on all former occasions, dictated to their sovereign, who had now dared even to hesitate in complying with their demands. They therefore immediately appointed a deputation of their most influential persons to proceed to the Sultan with their peremptory and absolute order, which insisted on the abolition of all the proposed innovations, and the giving up to their vengeance [of] all those who had advised or favoured them: and the deputation set out to execute their commission. It so happened that Kara Gehenem[2] had just before arrived, and having notice of this deputation, immediately proceeded to meet it with a corps of flying horse-artillery; he met them in the street as they were advancing, without the slightest suspicion of any hostile encounter, and instantly attacked them; the whole of this deputation, with a numerous body that accompanied it, were nearly destroyed on the spot, scarcely one having escaped. . . .

A last expedient was now resorted to, which at once decided the fate of the insurgents. The sangiak sheriff, or sacred standard of Mahomet, was brought forth with great pomp from its depository, to the enclosure of Sultan Achmet, surrounded by an immense concourse of people. Here the Sultan advanced, and, from the foot of the standard, he issued a solemn proclamation, detailing the faithless conduct of the janissaries, their solemn engagements under their hands and seals ten days before,[3] and their perjured violation of them. . . .

About three in the day, the numbers assembled round the sacred standard amounted to sixty thousand men; and the Sultan, now finding himself above all apprehension as to the final result, thought it right to endeavour to persuade the insurgents to lay down their arms and disperse. To this end more than one deputation was despatched to them, to state their hopeless opposition, and promise their lives to all who submitted; but the janissaries, as ignorant of what was going on outside their Etmeidan as if it was in another country, attributed these proposals to fear, and insolently rejected them, reiterating their former demands with menaces of vengeance. It was then resolved to resort to the last expedient, and reduce them with grape-shot. As a fit instrument for this purpose, Hussein, whose unpitying nature was already displayed, was appointed seraskier, or generalissimo, and the absolute command of the city and all its forces entrusted to him, to act against the insurgents. This commission was backed by a fetva, or ecclesiastical sentence of the mufti, and confirmed by a commission signed in

[2] 'The Black Infernal', Kara Husein Pasha. He was governor of Brusa and Ismid, commander of the Bosphorus forts and their garrisons, and the leader of the military forces loyal to Mahmud II in Constantinople.

[3] On 29 May representatives of the janissaries had agreed in writing to accept the Sultan's military reforms.

haste by the Sultan on the spot. The seraskier advanced with his artillery against the Etmeidan, where the janissaries were crowded together in blind confidence on [sic] their numbers, and total ignorance of the state of their opponents. Indeed the gross neglect and imbecility of the janissaries on this trying occasion, when it might be expected that all the talent, knowledge, and energy of the body would be put forth, is a proof what worthless and inefficient soldiers they must have been, and how necessary was [sic] the proposed changes. They made no disposition to occupy favourable places, to seize the city gates behind them, and keep their communication open with the country, but they quietly suffered themselves to be surrounded on all sides, and their retreat cut off in every quarter. It was said, indeed, that the great mass were still persuaded that no soldiers would dare to oppose them; and when the crisis actually arrived, that any body of troops which advanced to the Etmeidan would do so only to join their standards. Those who were in the middle of the crowd still spoke with a blind and insolent exultation, and made no movement, as if they thought none was necessary; but those who were nearest the street and observed the topgees with their artillery close on them, and ready to discharge their guns, made a sudden and simultaneous rush through the different avenues which led from the Etmeidan. The topgees seeing the dense mass approach, and feeling perhaps the yearnings which were supposed to be very general among the Turks for this corps, and those compunctions which every Mahomedan has in drawing his sword against his brethren of the same creed, were now observed to hesitate, and there was a probability that the blind security and confidence of the rabble in the sympathy of their brethren would be justified. It was the intention of the janissaries to seize the guns and turn them on their adversaries. The topgees drew back with their linstocks, and in a few minutes more their own artillery would have been thundering down the street after them. In this emergency Kara Gehenem rushed forward, and having no other means to ignite the powder, he discharged his pistol into the touch-hole of one of the pieces. The hands of the foremost janissaries were nearly on the muzzle of the gun when the discharge took place – the carnage was terrible – the street was crowded from side to side by a dense mass pushing one another on, and nearly the whole were in a moment struck down; the remainder hesitated, then turned back, and rushed again to the Etmeidan, where they were immediately followed by the artillery. They now dispersed in different directions, and finally took refuge in their kishlas or barracks.

And now Hussein, who for the first time, it is said, felt the smallest desire to show mercy to his former associates, sent a despatch to the Sultan to report the state of things, and take his further orders, before he proceeded to the last extremity. The Sultan immediately returned a hatta sheriff, directing him to surround the barracks, set fire to the buildings, and destroy with grape-shot all who had taken refuge within. The topgees, the bostangees, and the seymans were appointed for this service. The janissaries entrenched behind the walls of their barracks, and, animated by despair, made here a fierce resistance. . . . All mercy was now withdrawn – no quarter was given – the artillery continued to play on the blazing buildings; every one who attempted to escape was driven back, or massacred on the spot, and six thousand mangled and scorched bodies were next day found among the smoking ruins.

Every care had been taken to guard strongly the gates of the city, as well to cut off all communication with the janissaries without, as to prevent those within from escaping the vigilance of the police, who were everywhere on the alert to apprehend them. It was then the more horrible work of destruction began, because it was a massacre in cold blood; domiciliary visits were made in every place, and whenever a janissary was met in the streets, or found in a house, he was instantly put to death without pity or remorse, and his body cast into the kennel; and before the middle of the next day, besides the five [sic] thousand mangled carcasses lying among the burnt kishlas, there were as many more weltering in the streets of every part or the city, so as in some places to stop up the passage.

[This slaughter continued for some time, until it was thought advisable to call a halt.] As the determination was to extirpate the very name of this devoted corps, and not leave a man behind who bore it, it was now resolved not to kill but to banish the survivors, and to send out at the same time every useless or suspected person. A number of people had latterly left their residence in Asia, and had flocked to the capital to seek employment, the great body of the hummals or porters, the trombagees or firemen, the ciaquegees or boatmen, the Albanians who attended the public baths, the common bakers, and sundry others, were of this description. These men were taken up, and sent by detachments of one hundred at a time, across to Scutari, and so to different towns in Asia, with strict orders to the pashas that they should never grant them a teskerai, or permit, again to return to the city. For six weeks these detachments were sent off every day, till at length, in this way, no less than ten thousand persons, including the families of the exiles, were compelled to leave the city. It is supposed that about ten thousand persons in all were killed in the conflict, and that the suppression of the janissaries caused a loss of population to the city of twenty thousand individuals in about six weeks.

R. Walsh, *A Residence at Constantinople during a Period including the Commencement, Progress, and Termination of the Greek and Turkish Revolutions* (London, 1836), ii, 509-17

3 The Hatt-i Sherif of Gulhané, 3 November 1839

This famous decree was issued at a moment when much of the Empire seemed about to be overrun by the armies of Mehemet Ali (see **IV, 5, 6** above) and was intended largely to show the European powers that the Porte as well as the Pasha of Egypt could govern along liberal and modern lines. The frank recognition of the need to create 'new institutions' and the provision that members of different religious groups should be equal before the law both represented a radical, and to many Turks shocking, breach with Muslim principles and traditions. The decree inaugurated the period of *Tanzimat* (reorganization) in the Ottoman Empire which can be seen as continuing until the promulgation of the constitution of 1876.

Everyone knows that, in the early years of the Ottoman monarchy' the glorious precepts of the Koran and the laws of the Empire were a rule always held in honour. As a result, the Empire grew in strength and greatness, and all its subjects, without exception, had reached the highest degree of ease and prosperity. For the last hundred and fifty years a series of accidents and different causes have meant that we have ceased to observe the sacred Code of the laws and the regulations derived from it, and the former strength and prosperity have changed into weakness and impoverishment; this is because in fact an Empire loses all stability when it ceases to observe its laws.

These considerations are continually present in our mind, and, from the day of our accession to the throne, the thought of the public good, of the improvement of the condition of the provinces and of the relief of our peoples, has not ceased to occupy it to the exclusion of all else. But, if we consider the geographical position of the Ottoman provinces, the fertility of the soil, the aptitude and intelligence of the inhabitants, we shall be convinced that if we apply ourselves to finding effective remedies the result, which with the help of God we hope to achieve, can be obtained within a few years. Thus, full of confidence in the aid of the Most High, supported by the intercession of our Prophet, we consider it appropriate to seek by new institutions to procure for the provinces which make up the Ottoman Empire the benefit of a good administration.

These institutions should relate principally to three points, which are:

First. The guarantees which assure to our subjects complete security for their lives, their honour and their fortune.

Second. A regular method of assessing and levying taxes.

Third. An equally regular method for the raising of soldiers and the length of their service.

And, in fact, are not life and honour the most precious goods which exist? What man, however great the distaste for violence with which his character inspires him, can restrain himself from having recourse to it and thus injuring the Government and the country, if his life and honour are placed in danger? If, on the other hand, he enjoys in this respect perfect security, he will not forsake the paths of loyalty and all his acts will contribute to the well-being of the Government and of his brothers.

If there is an absence of security with regard to property, everyone remains unresponsive to the voice of the Prince and of the fatherland; no one cares for the public good, absorbed as all are by their own anxieties. If, on the contrary, the citizen possesses with confidence his property of all kinds, then [he is] full of ardour in the pursuit of his own business, the scope of which he seeks to enlarge so as to extend that of his pleasures, which every day redouble in his heart love of his Prince and of the fatherland, and devotion to his country. In him these feelings become the source of the most praiseworthy actions.

As for the regular and fixed assessment of taxation, it is very important to settle this matter, for the State, which for the defence of its territory is forced to incur various expenses, cannot obtain the money needed for its armies and other services except by contributions levied on its subjects. Although, thank God, those of our Empire have for some time been freed from the scourge of monopolies, which used mistakenly to be regarded as a source of revenue, a destructive custom still persists, although it can have only disastrous consequences; it is that of the sale of concessions known under the name of *iltizam*. Under this system the civil and financial administration of a locality is placed under the arbitrary control of a single man, that is to say, sometimes under the iron hand of the most violent and greedy passions, for if this farmer is not good he will have no care for anything but his own advantage.

It is thus necessary that henceforth each member of Ottoman society should be assessed for a fixed and determined amount of taxation, depending on his fortune and his abilities, and that nothing more can be demanded of him. It is necessary also that special laws should fix and limit the expenses of our land and sea forces.

Although, as we have said, the defence of the country is a matter of importance, and that it is a duty for all the inhabitants to supply soldiers for this purpose, it has become necessary to establish laws to regulate the contingents which each locality, according to the necessity of the moment, must provide, and to reduce to four or five years the period of military service. For to take, without regard to the respective population of different areas, from one more, and from another fewer, men than they can supply, is simultaneously to do an injustice and strike a mortal blow at agriculture and industry; in the same way to keep soldiers in the service for the whole of their lives is to reduce them to despair and contribute to the depopulation of the countryside.

In sum, without the different laws whose necessity has just been seen the Empire can have neither strength, nor riches, nor happiness, nor tranquillity; these must, on the contrary, be looked for from the existence of these new laws.

This is why henceforth the case of every accused shall be judged publicly, in conformity with our divine law, after an enquiry and examination, and as long as no regular judgement has been given, no one shall be able, secretly or publicly, to put to death another by poison or by any other means.

It shall not be allowed to any person to injure the honour of any other whatsoever.

Everyone shall possess his property of all kinds, and shall dispose of it with the most complete liberty, without anyone being able to prevent this; thus, for example, the innocent heirs of a criminal shall not be deprived of their legal rights and the goods of the criminal shall not be confiscated.

These imperial concessions extend to all our subjects, of whatever religion or sect they may be; they shall enjoy them without exception. Perfect security is thus granted by us to the inhabitants of the Empire, in their life, their honour and their possessions, as is demanded by the sacred text of our law.

As to the other points, as they must be settled by the agreement of enlightened opinions, our Council of Justice (augmented by new members, in so far as this may be necessary) which shall be joined, on certain days which we shall decide, by our Ministers and the notables of the Empire, shall assemble in order to establish laws regulating these points of security of life and property, and that of the assessment of taxation. In these assemblies each member shall freely express his ideas and give his opinion.

The laws concerning the regularization of military service shall be debated in the Military Council, sitting at the palace of the Seraskier.

As soon as a law has been drawn up, to be for ever valid and in force, it shall be presented to us; we shall embellish it with our sanction, which we shall write at its head with our imperial hand.

As these present institutions have as their object only to produce a revival of religion, the Government, the Nation and the Empire, we undertake to do nothing which shall be contrary to them. As a guarantee of our promise, we wish, after having deposited them in the chamber which contains the glorious mantle of the Prophet, in presence of all the ulema and great men of the Empire, to take an oath in the name of God and to make the ulema and the great men of the Empire then swear an oath.

After this, any of the ulema or great men of the Empire, or any other person whatever, who shall violate these institutions shall suffer, without regard to rank, status or influence, the penalty corresponding to his offence, when the latter has been clearly proved. A penal Code shall be drawn up to this effect.

As all the officials of the Empire today receive a suitable salary, and as the payment of those whose functions are not yet sufficiently remunerated shall be regularized, a rigorous law shall be directed against traffic in favours and posts which is reproved by the divine law and which is one of the principal causes of the decadence of the Empire.

The provisions drawn up above being an alteration and complete renovation of ancient usages, this imperial rescript shall be published at Constantinople and in all the places of our Empire, and shall be communicated officially to all the ambassadors of friendly Powers residing at Constantinople, that they may be witnesses of the grant of these institutions, which, if God pleases, shall endure for ever.

May God the All-Highest have us all in his holy and worthy keeping.

May those who shall perform an act contrary to the present laws be the object of divine malediction and for ever deprived of every form of happiness.

G. Young, Corps de Droit Ottoman (Oxford, 1905-6), i, 29-33

4   The Hatt-i Humayun of 18 February 1856

Drawn up as part of the preliminaries to the signature of the peace of Paris (**VI, 9** below), this decree, like the Hatt-i Sherif of Gulhané (**V, 3** above) was intended to show the powers of Europe that the Ottoman Empire could and would effectively modernize its administrative and even its social structure. It is a reaffirmation, in a rather more specific form, of the principles laid down in the decree of 1839. Notice once more the emphasis on equality of rights and obligations between Christians and Muslims in the empire; though in this respect the gap between promise and performance continued to be wide for long after 1856.

1. The guarantees promised on our part to all the subjects of my Empire by the Hatti-Hamayoun of Gulhané, and in conformity with the Tanzimat, without distinction of classes or religion, for the security of their persons and property, and the preservation of their honour, are today confirmed and consolidated, and efficacious measures shall be taken in order that they may have their full and entire effect.

2. All the privileges and spiritual immunities granted by my ancestors *ab antiquo*, and at subsequent dates, to all Christian communities or other non-Mussulman religious groups established in my Empire, under my protection, shall be confirmed and maintained.

3. Every Christian or other non-Mussulman community shall be bound within a fixed period, and with the concurrence of a commission composed *ad hoc* of its own members, to proceed, with my high approbation and under the inspection of my Sublime Porte, to examine its present immunities and privileges, and to discuss and submit to my Sublime Porte the reforms required by the progress of enlightenment and of the age. The powers conceded to the Christian patriarchs and bishops by the Sultan Mohamed II and his successors shall be made to harmonize with the new position which my generous and beneficent intentions assure to these communities. The principle of nominating the Patriarchs for life, after the revision of the rule of election now in force, shall be exactly carried out, in conformity with the tenor of their firmans of investiture. The Patriarchs, metropolitans, archbishops, bishops, and rabbins shall take an oath, on their entrance into office, according to a form agreed upon in common by my Sublime Porte and the spiritual heads of the different religious communities. . . .

7. . . . My Sublime Porte will take energetic measures to ensure to

each religious group, whatever be the number of its adherents, entire freedom in the exercise of its religion.

8. Every distinction or designation tending to make any class whatever of the subjects of my Empire inferior to another class, on account of their religion, language, or race, shall be forever effaced from administrative protocol. The laws shall be put in force against the use of any injurious or offensive term either among private individuals or on the part of the authorities.

9. As all forms of religion are and shall be freely professed in my dominions, no subject of my Empire shall be hindered in the exercise of the religion that he professes, nor shall he be in any way annoyed on this account. No one shall be compelled to change his religion.

10. The nomination and choice of all functionaries and other employees of my Empire being entirely dependent upon my sovereign will, all the subjects of my Empire, without distinction of nationality, shall be admissible to public employments, and qualified to fill them, according to their capacity and merit, and conformably with rules to be generally applied.

11. All the subjects of my Empire shall be received without discrimination into the civil and military schools of the Government, if they otherwise satisfy the conditions as to age and examination which are specified in the organic regulations of the said schools.

12. All commercial, correctional, and criminal suits between Mussulmans and Christians, or other non-Mussulman subjects, or between Christians or other non-Mussulmans of different sects, shall be referred to mixed Tribunals.

The proceedings of these Tribunals shall be public; the parties shall be confronted with each other and shall produce their witnesses, whose testimony shall be received without discrimination, upon an oath to be taken according to the religious law of each sect. . . .

13. Penal, correctional, and commercial laws, and rules of procedure to be applied to the mixed tribunals, shall be drawn up as soon as possible and codified. Translations of them shall be published in all the languages in use in the Empire. . . .

15. The organization of the police in the capital, in the provincial towns, and in the rural districts, shall be revised in such a manner as to

give to all the peaceable subjects of my Empire the strongest guarantees for the safety both of their persons and property.

16. The equality of taxes entailing equality of burdens, as equality of duties entails that of rights, Christian subjects, and those of other non-Mussulman sects, as it has been already decided, shall, as well as Mussulmans, be subject to the obligations of the law of recruitment. . . .

18. As the laws regulating the purchase, sale, and disposal of real property are common to all the subjects of my Empire, it shall be lawful for foreigners to possess landed property in my dominions if they observe the laws and police regulations, and bear the same charges as the native inhabitants, and after arrangements have been come to with foreign Powers.

19. Taxes are to be levied on the same basis from all the subjects of my Empire, without distinction of class or religion. The most prompt and energetic means for remedying the abuses in collecting the taxes, and especially the tithes, shall be considered. The system of direct collection shall gradually, and as soon as possible, be substituted for the plan of farming, in all branches of the revenues of the state. . . .

21. As a special law has already been passed, which orders that the budget of the state revenue and expenditure shall be drawn up and made known every year, the said law shall be most scrupulously observed. Action shall be taken to revise the salaries attached to each office.

22. The heads of each community and a delegate, designated by my Sublime Porte, shall be summoned to take part in the deliberations of the supreme Council of Justice in all circumstances which may interest the generality of the subjects of my Empire. They shall be summoned specially for this purpose by my Grand Vizier. The delegates shall hold office for one year; they shall take an oath on entering upon their duties. All the members of the Council, at the ordinary and extraordinary meetings, shall freely give their opinions and their votes, and no one shall ever give them anxiety on this account.

G. Young, *Corps de Droit Ottoman* (Oxford, 1905-6), ii, 4-9

VI

THE CRIMEAN WAR

1   The 'Nesselrode Memorandum', 3 December 1844

This memorandum was drawn up by Count Nesselrode, the Russian Chancellor, during a visit to England in September 1844 and was submitted to the British government on 3 December. It summarizes a verbal agreement arrived at early in June in conversations between Nicholas I on the one hand and Sir Robert Peel (the Prime Minister) and Lord Aberdeen (the Foreign Secretary) on the other, when the Tsar visited England. Nicholas, imbued with the idea that the collapse of the Ottoman Empire was certain and that agreements with Austria and Britain for the disposal of its territories were essential, failed to realise that he had not persuaded the British government to accept a binding and permanent commitment. This misunderstanding probably encouraged him later to pursue the policies which led to the outbreak of the Crimean War.

Russia and England are mutually penetrated with the conviction that it is for their common interest that the Ottoman Porte should maintain itself in the state of independence and of territorial possession which at present constitutes that Empire, as that political combination is the one which is most compatible with the general interest of the maintenance of peace.

Being agreed on this principle, Russia and England have an equal interest in uniting their efforts in order to keep up the existence of the Ottoman Empire, and to avert all the dangers which can place in jeopardy its safety.

With this object the essential point is to suffer the Porte to live in repose, without needlessly disturbing it by diplomatic bickerings, and without interfering without absolute necessity in its internal affairs.

[However the Porte should not be allowed, by playing on the jealousies of the powers, to escape its treaty obligations. It must also be prevented from ill-treating its Christian subjects.]

In the uncertainty which hovers over the future, a single fundamental idea seems to admit of a really practical application; it is that the danger which may result from a catastrophe in Turkey will be much diminished, if, in the event of its occurring, Russia and England have come to an understanding as to the course to be taken by them in common.

That understanding will be the more beneficial, inasmuch as it will have the full assent of Austria. Between her and Russia there exists already an entire conformity of principles in regard to the affairs of Turkey, in a common interest of conservatism and of peace.

In order to render their union more efficacious, there would remain nothing to be desired but that England should be seen to associate herself thereto with the same view.

The reason which recommends the establishment of this agreement is very simple.

On land Russia exercises in regard to Turkey a preponderant action. On sea England occupies the same position.

Isolated, the action of these two Powers might do much mischief. United, it can produce a real benefit; thence, the advantage of coming to a previous understanding before having recourse to action.

This notion was in principle agreed upon during the Emperor's last residence in London. The result was the eventual engagement, that if anything unforeseen occurred in Turkey, Russia and England should previously concert together as to the course which they should pursue in common.

The object for which Russia and England will have to come to an understanding may be expressed in the following manner:

1. To seek to maintain the existence of the Ottoman Empire in its present state, so long as that political combination shall be possible.

2. If we foresee that it must crumble to pieces, to enter into previous concert as to everything relating to the establishment of a new order of things, intended to replace that which now exists, and in conjunction with each other to see that the change which may have occurred in the internal situation of that Empire shall not injuriously affect either the security of their own States and the rights which the Treaties assure to them respectively, or the maintenance of the balance of power in Europe.

For the purpose thus stated, the policy of Russia and Austria, as we have already said, is closely united by the principle of perfect identity. If England, as the principal Maritime Power, acts in concert with them, t is to be supposed that France will find herself obliged to act in conformity with the course agreed upon between St. Petersburgh, London, and Vienna.

Conflict between the Great Powers being thus obviated, it is to be hoped that the peace of Europe will be maintained even in the midst of such serious circumstances. It is to secure this object of common interest, if the case occurs, that, as the Emperor agreed with Her Britannic Majesty's Ministers during his residence in England, the previous understanding which Russia and England shall establish between themselves must be directed.

A. and P., 1854, lxxi Pt. VI, pp. 2-4

2 Nicholas I considers Russian Policy in the Near East, early 1853

These brief notes, drawn up by the Tsar at the beginning of 1853, are interesting as showing his continuing indecision as to the policy which Russia should pursue towards the Ottoman Empire. They also make it clear, however, that he envisaged as at least a possibility a Russo-Turkish war followed by the seizure of much Turkish territory by Russia, Austria and Britain.

Autograph Note of the Emperor Nicholas I concerning the Eastern Question before the mission of Menshikov, 1853

What should be our objective?
1. Reparation.
2. Guarantees for the future. What form can they take?
3. Conservation of the position as it used to be. Is this probable?

What are the means of attaining our objective?
1. Negotiations:
   a) by letter
   b) by the sending of an embassy. Advantages and drawbacks.
2. Intimidation by recall of our mission. Drawbacks.
3. By force:
   a) declaration of war. Drawbacks;
   b) surprise by occupation of the principalities. Drawbacks;
   c) surprise attack on Constantinople. Advantages, drawbacks; chances of success.

Probable results:
1. Turkey will give way.
2. She will not give way; destruction of Constantinople.
3. The defeated Turkish army retreats towards Gallipoli or Enos.

4. Occupation of the Dardanelles.
5. The French send a fleet and an expeditionary force. Conflicts with them.

Chances of success; possibility of setbacks:

6. We have the upper hand, Constantinople and the Dardanelles are in our hands, the Turkish army is routed.
7. Fall of the Ottoman Empire.
8. Should we reestablish it and on what conditions?
9. Can we reestablish it with a chance of success?
10. With what should it be replaced?
   a) Keep all its European territory. Impossible.
   b) Keep Constantinople and the Dardanelles – disadvantages.
   c) Constantinople alone – an impossibility.
   d) Division into independent provinces.
   e) Reestablishment of the Byzantine Empire.
   f) Reunion with Greece.
      Impossibility of both.
   g) Division between ourselves, Austria, England and France.
   h) What to do with Constantinople.
   i) The least bad of all bad solutions.
   a) The Principalities and Bulgaria as far as Kistendji to Russia.
   b) Serbia and Bulgaria independent.
   c) The coasts of the Archipelago and the Adriatic to Austria.
   d) Egypt to England: perhaps Cyprus and Rhodes.
   e) Crete to France.
   f) The islands of the Archipelago to Greece.
   g) Constantinople a free city; the Bosphorus Russian garrison; the Dardanelles Austrian garrison.
   h) Complete freedom of trade.
   i) The Turkish Empire in Asia Minor.

Zaionchkovskii, i, 357-8

3 Nesselrode envisages a Rupture of Russo-Turkish Relations, 9 February 1853

The idea of sending a special Russian embassy to Constantinople to secure satisfaction for Russia's demands with relation to the Holy Places originated with Nesselrode, not with Nicholas I, and the unsuccessful Menshikov mission was a decisive step in the sequence of events which produced the Crimean War. This extract from Menshikov's instructions shows the potentially dangerous determination of the Russian government to impose the heaviest possible diplomatic pressure on the Turks.

Count Nesselrode to Prince Menshikov, 9 February 1853

If the blindness of the men who today govern Turkey were pushed to such a point [i.e. that of refusing or eluding Russia's demands] and if the fear of displeasing France led them to neglect all other considerations even at the risk of provoking a rupture with Russia, in such a case it would become useless to prolong the negotiation and the discussions. Your Excellency would have only one last action to take. You would demand of the Grand Vizier a solemn audience to receive from you a communication of very high importance.

After a short exposition of the engagements undertaken by the Porte towards Russia, engagements of which Your Excellency will have in your hands the evidence, including the letter written last year to the Emperor by the Sultan, you will declare that as long as the firman and the Hatti-Sherif, by which the state of affairs established at Jerusalem was finally confirmed, are not loyally and *literally* enforced, the imperial court cannot, without sacrificing its dignity and exposing itself to new offences, continue to have a mission at Constantinople and to carry on on the old footing its political relations with the Ottoman government; that as a result and in virtue of the full powers with which Your Excellency is provided, you will leave Constantinople, taking with you all the personnel of the imperial legation except the director of the commercial chancery who will continue to transact business relating to navigation and commerce and to protect the interests of Russian subjects and the passage of our ships; that you regret profoundly to have to take this decision, but that after having faithfully carried out the orders of the Emperor and submitted to the consideration of the Porte the most conciliatory proposals, those most equitable and even most in conformity with the real interests of the Ottoman Empire, you have acquired the painful certainty that there was little readiness to welcome them and do them justice; that therefore you are fulfilling a final duty in protesting in the presence of the principal functionaries of the Empire and in throwing all the responsibility for the consequences which may arise on those ministers of the Sultan who have recently laboured to produce a serious misunderstanding between their government and Russia.

Before leaving the audience, Your Excellency will hand to the Grand Vizier an official note, drawn up in the sense of the verbal declaration which has just been sketched here and of which you can modify the terms, according to what you consider necessary, depending on the course which the negotiation has taken and the more or less flagrant proofs of bad faith which the Turkish ministry has given.

Three days after the presentation of this note, Your Excellency can leave Constantinople, giving M. Ozeroff[1] orders to follow quickly with the personnel of the legation except for the dragoman and the first secretary who will continue there without functions or diplomatic character, but who will be considered as helping the director of the commercial chancery in the handling of the current business of merchants and sailors who are Russian subjects.

Zaionchkovskii, i, 375

4 The Seymour Conversations, January-February 1853

These conversations are the best example of the dangerous belief of Nicholas I in personal and informal diplomacy. There is no doubt of the sincerity of his desire for an agreement with Great Britain; but he completely failed to understand how difficult it was for a parliamentary government to give him the informal gentleman's agreement for which he was asking, and the effect of the conversations was to make both Seymour, the British ambassador in St. Petersburg, and Russell, the Foreign Secretary, increasingly and perhaps unduly suspicious of his intentions.

(a) *Sir G. H. Seymour to Lord John Russell, 22 January 1853 (reporting on a conversation of 14 January)*

I found His Majesty alone; he received me with great kindness, saying that I had appeared desirous to speak to him upon Eastern affairs; that, on his side, there was no indisposition to do so, but that he must begin at a remote period.

You know, His Majesty said, the dreams and plans in which the Empress Catherine was in the habit of indulging; these were handed down to our time; but while I inherited immense territorial possessions, I did not inherit those visions, those intentions if you like to call them so. On the contrary, my country is so vast, so happily circumstanced in every way, that it would be unreasonable in me to desire more territory or more power than I possess; on the contrary, I am the first to tell you that our great, perhaps our only danger, is that

[1] The Russian chargé d'affaires.

which would arise from an extension given to an Empire already too large.

Close to us lies Turkey, and in our present condition, nothing better for our interests can be desired; the times have gone by when we had anything to fear from the fanatical spirit or the military enterprise of the Turks, and yet the country is strong enough, or has hitherto been strong enough, to preserve its independence, and to insure respectful treatment from other countries.

Well, in that Empire there are several millions of Christians whose interests I am called upon to watch over, while the right of doing so is secured to me by Treaty. I may truly say that I make a moderate and sparing use of my right, and I will freely confess that it is one which is attended with obligations occasionally very inconvenient; but I cannot recede from the discharge of a distinct duty. Our religion, as established in this country, came to us from the East, and there are feelings, as well as obligations, which never must be lost sight of.

Now Turkey, in the condition which I have described, has by degrees fallen into such a state of decrepitude that, as I told you the other night, eager as we all are for the continued existence of the man (and that I am as desirous as you can be for the continuance of his life, I beg you to believe), he may suddenly die upon our hands; we cannot resuscitate what is dead; if the Turkish Empire falls, it falls to rise no more; and I put it to you, therefore, whether it is not better to be provided beforehand for a contingency, than to incur the chaos, confusion, and the certainty of an European war, all of which must attend the catastrophe if it should occur unexpectedly, and before some ulterior system has been sketched; this is the point to which I am desirous that you should call the attention of your Government.

Sir, I replied, your Majesty is so frank with me, that I am sure you will have the goodness to permit me to speak with the same openness. I would then observe, that deplorable as is the condition of Turkey, it is a country which has long been plunged in difficulties supposed by many to be insurmountable.

With regard to contingent arrangements, Her Majesty's Government, as your Majesty is well aware, objects, as a general rule, to taking engagements upon possible eventualities, and would, perhaps, be particularly disinclined to doing so in this instance. If I may be allowed to say so, a great disinclination might be expected in England, to disposing by anticipation of the succession of an old friend and ally.

The rule is a good one, the Emperor replied, good at all times, especially in times of uncertainty and change, like the present; still it is of the greatest importance that we should understand one another, and not allow events to take us by surprise[2]; 'now I wish to speak to you as a friend and as a gentleman; if we manage to come to an understanding on this matter, England and I, for the rest, it matters little to me; I am indifferent as to what others do or think. Speaking frankly therefore, I tell you clearly, that if England dreams of one of these days establishing herself at Constantinople, I will not allow it; I do not attribute these intentions to you by any means, but on these occasions it is better to speak clearly. For my part, I am equally disposed to undertake not to establish myself there, as owner, be it understood, for as to temporary possession I say nothing; it could happen that circumstances put me in the position of occupying Constantinople, if nothing has been foreseen, if we must leave everything to chance. . . .

I am bound to say, that if words, tone and manner offer any criterion by which intentions are to be judged, the Emperor is prepared to act with perfect fairness and openness towards Her Majesty's Government. His Majesty has, no doubt, his own objects in view; and he is, in my opinion, too strong a believer in the imminence of dangers in Turkey. I am, however, impressed with the belief, that in carrying out those objects, as in guarding against those dangers, His Majesty is sincerely desirous of acting in harmony with Her Majesty's Government.

A. and P., 1854, lxxi Pt. V [1736], pp. 3–5

(b) *Lord John Russell to Sir G. H. Seymour, 9 February 1853*

In considering this grave question, the first reflection that occurs to Her Majesty's Government is that no actual crisis has occurred which renders necessary a solution of this vast European problem. Disputes have arisen concerning the Holy Places, but these are without the sphere of the internal government of Turkey, and concern Russia and France rather than the Sublime Porte. Some disturbance of the relations between Austria and the Porte has been caused by the Turkish attack on Montenegro[3]; but this, again, relates rather to dangers affecting the frontier of Austria than the authority and safety of the Sultan; so that there is no sufficient cause for intimating to the Sultan that he cannot keep peace at home, or preserve friendly relations with his neighbours.

It occurs further to Her Majesty's Government to remark, that the event which is contemplated is not definitely fixed in point of time. . . .

---

[2] The remainder of this paragraph is left in French in the original.
[3] Omer Pasha, the Turkish governor of Bosnia, had on his own initiative declared war on Montenegro at the end of 1852.

In these circumstances it would hardly be consistent with the friendly feelings towards the Sultan which animate the Emperor of Russia, no less than the Queen of Great Britain, to dispose beforehand of the provinces under his dominion. Besides this consideration, however, it must be observed, that an agreement made in such a case tends very surely to hasten the contingency for which it is intended to provide. Austria and France could not, in fairness, be kept in ignorance of the transaction, nor would such concealment be consistent with the end of preventing an European war. Indeed, such concealment cannot be intended by His Imperial Majesty. It is to be inferred that, as as soon as Great Britain and Russia should have agreed on the course to be pursued, and have determined to enforce it, they should communicate their intentions to the Great Powers of Europe. An agreement thus made, and thus communicated, would not be very long a secret; and while it would alarm and alienate the Sultan, the knowledge of its existence would stimulate all his enemies to increased violence and more obstinate conflict. They would fight with the conviction that they must ultimately triumph; while the Sultan's generals and troops would feel that no immediate success could save their cause from final overthrow. Thus would be produced and strengthened that very anarchy which is now feared, and the foresight of the friends of the patient would prove the cause of his death. . . .

Upon the whole, then, Her Majesty's Government are persuaded that no course of policy can be adopted more wise, more disinterested, more beneficial to Europe than that which His Imperial Majesty has so long followed, and which will render his name more illustrious than that of the most famous Sovereigns who have sought immortality by unprovoked conquest and ephemeral glory.

A. and P., 1854, lxxi Pt. V, pp. 6-8

5 Nesselrode on the Position in the Near East, 5 March 1853

Here the Russian Chancellor defends the action of the Tsar in embarking on the conversations with Seymour (see **VI, 4** above), though he had himself advised Nicholas against this attempt at agreement with Britain. He also states the Russian case against France as the disturber of the peace and of established rights in the Near East.

Note Verbale of Nesselrode to Seymour, 5 March 1853

In conversing familiarly with the British envoy on the causes which, from one day to the next, may bring about the fall of the Ottoman Empire, the Emperor never thought at all of proposing, for this eventuality, a plan by which Russia and England would dispose in advance of the provinces ruled by the Sultan, a ready-made system, still less a formal transaction to be concluded between the two cabinets. In the mind of the Emperor it was a matter purely and simply of expressing confidentially on both sides, less what was wanted *than what was not wanted*; what would be contrary to English interests; what would be contrary to Russian interests; so that, if the case arose, each side could avoid actions *which contradicted those of the other*.

This does not involve either schemes of partition or an agreement to be forced on other courts. It is a simple exchange of opinions, and the Emperor does not see any need to talk of it prematurely. It is precisely for this reason that he has taken care not to suggest making it the object of an official communication from Cabinet to Cabinet. In limiting himself to personal discussion, under the form of a private conversation, with the representative of the Queen, he has chosen the most intimate and confidential method of revealing his ideas frankly to Her Britannic Majesty, desiring that any result of these discussions should remain what it ought to be, a secret between the two Sovereigns . . .

In presence of the uncertainty and weakness of the present state of affairs in Turkey, the English Cabinet expresses the desire that the greatest patience should be exercised towards the Porte. The Emperor is not conscious of ever having acted otherwise. The English Cabinet itself agrees on this. It has addressed to the Emperor, on the numerous proofs of his moderation which he has given to this day, praise which His Majesty cannot accept since he has done nothing but obey in this his own dominant convictions. But so that the Emperor should be able to continue to agree to this policy of patience – to abstain from all demonstrations, from peremptory language – it is necessary that this system be followed simultaneously by all the Powers. France has adopted a different one. It is through threats that she has obtained, against the letter of the treaties, the admission of a warship into the Dardanelles.[4] It is at the mouth of cannon that she has twice put forward

---

[4] In May 1852 the Sultan had been forced to allow a French warship, the *Charlemagne*, to pass through the Dardanelles *en route* for Constantinople. Since it carried the French ambassador its passage was not technically a breach of the Straits Convention.

claims and demands for compensation at Tripoli,[5] then at Constanti-nople. Again it is by intimidation that, in the contest over the Holy Places, she has brought about the anullment of the firman and of solemn promises which the Sultan had given the Emperor. In face of all these acts of overweening power England has kept complete silence. She has made neither offers of support to the Porte nor remonstrances to the French government. The result is perfectly clear. The Porte has drawn the necessary conclusion that it was from France alone that she had everything to hope or fear, and that she could with impunity evade the claims of Austria and Russia. It is thus that Russia and Austria, to obtain justice, have seen themselves in their turn, against their will, forced to act by intimidation, since they have to deal with a govern-ment which gives way only in face of a peremptory attitude; and it is thus that through its own faults, or rather through that of those who have first of all weakened it, the Porte is driven into a course of action which weakens it still further. Let England then exert herself to make it see reason. In place of uniting with France against the just claims of Russia, let her take care not to support or even to appear to support the resistance of the Ottoman government. Let her be the first to invite the latter, as she herself thinks is essential, to treat its Christian subjects with more fairness and humanity. This will be the surest way of sparing the Emperor the obligation of exerting in Turkey those traditional rights of protection which he uses only unwillingly, and to postpone indefinitely the crisis which the Emperor and Her Majesty the Queen are equally anxious to guard against.

Zaionchkovskii, i, 363-4

6 Urquhart on the Russian Menace to Europe

David Urquhart, who had fought in the Greek War of Independence and served in the British embassy at Constantinople in the 1830s, was a prolific writer on Near Eastern affairs and the most bitter, effective and extreme of all anti-Russian pamphleteers in Britain during the middle decades of the nine-teenth century. This extract is a good illustration of the exaggerated popular views of Russian power and malevolence which helped to push Britain into the Crimean War.

You have long been in a slumber, and she has profited by your security; you have long confided in her honour, she has profited by your friend-

---

[5] At the end of July 1852 a French naval squadron was sent to Tripoli to force the surrender of two French deserters who had taken refuge there.

ship; your eyes are at length opened, and your indignation aroused – does she suffer retribution, do you regain character? You discover that she is illogical – in rhetoric which has convulsed an Empire; you denounce her to be insane – in marching with your aid on the Bosphorus; you send your men-of-war to the Dardanelles – she seizes the Sound; she grasps the Danube – you send – no, you do *not* send, a note; she usurps the vastest plain of Europe, and you *do* send an apology. When she has overrun a province you convoke a conclave; you prevent war by removing landmarks; and stop a burglar by opening the door. And all this is peace; two campaigns and a dozen fortresses are offered up for the sake of the tranquillity of Europe; and two Empires[6] are stripped of their arms in the interest of their defence.

There remains, however, another discovery to be made – not that you are cowards, but that you are impostors. Was there ever imposition compared with that of your pretending to cope with Russia? She can be met only by men with minds equal to herself; equal to her in cunning, or at least superior to her in honesty; you have neither the last, nor do you form the first.   While she perverts truth and justice through love of power, you sacrifice right and power by fatuity. This is your struggle with Russia, or rather your confederacy. . . .

Treaties are to her the scaffolds by which she builds, as she ascends, she knocks them down. That of Vienna in 1815 gave her Poland, but did not prevent her, in 1846, from disposing of Cracow. That of Adrianople in 1829 gave her the mouths of the Danube on conditions, but does not prevent her, in 1853, from blocking up the entrance in violation of these conditions. That of Balta Liman, in 1849, gave her a conjoint occupation, for seven years, of the Principalities, but does not prevent her, in 1853, from assuming and practising a separate and exclusive occupation. So too that of London, in 1841, gave her the exclusion of foreign vessels of war from the Euxine on the condition of respecting the integrity of the Ottoman Empire, and so also it does not prevent her, in 1853, from violating that integrity.

David Urquhart, *Progress of Russia in the West, North and South*, 2nd ed. (London, 1853), Preface, pp. xviii–xix, xxxii–xxxiii

7   The 'Vienna Note', 1 August 1853

It was proposed by a conference of representatives of the great powers, meeting

[6] Turkey and Austria.

in Vienna, that this note should be addressed by the Porte to Russia. This was the most important of a number of efforts made during the late summer and autumn of 1853 to smooth over the increasing antagonism between Russia and the Ottoman Empire. However the Turkish Grand Council refused to accept the note unless it were modified to make it clear that the privileges of the Orthodox in the Ottoman Empire were based merely on concessions to them by the Sultan. The Russian government refused to accept this change, and it became clear that it interpreted the note as giving it a right of intervention in the Ottoman Empire in defence of the Orthodox and their rights. War thus became almost certain.

If the Emperors of Russia have at all times evinced their active solicitude for the maintenance of the immunities and privileges of the orthodox Greek Church in the Ottoman Empire, the Sultans have never refused again to confirm them by solemn acts testifying their ancient and constant benevolence towards their Christian subjects. His Majesty the Sultan, Abdul-Medjid, now reigning, inspired with the same dispositions, and being desirous of giving to His Majesty the Emperor of Russia a personal proof of his most sincere friendship, and of his hearty desire to consolidate the ancient relations of good neighbourhood and thorough understanding existing between the two States, has been solely influenced by his unbounded confidence in the eminent qualities of his august friend and ally, and has been pleased to take into serious consideration the representations which his Excellency Prince Menchikoff conveyed to him.

The Undersigned has in consequence received orders to declare by the present note that the Government of His Majesty the Sultan will remain faithful to the letter and to the spirit of the Treaties of Kainardji and Adrianople relative to the protection of the Christian religion, and that His Majesty considers himself bound in honour to cause to be observed for ever, and to preserve from all prejudice either now or hereafter, the enjoyment of the spiritual privileges which have been granted by His Majesty's august ancestors to the orthodox Eastern Church, and which are maintained and confirmed by him; and moreover, in a spirit of exalted equity, to cause the Greek rite to share in the advantages granted to the other Christian rites by Convention or special arrangement. . . .

The Sublime Porte, moreover, officially promises that the existing state of things shall in no wise be modified without previous understanding with the Governments of France and Russia, and without any prejudice to the different Christian communities.

A. and P., 1854, lxxi Pt. II, pp. 26-7

8   Russia decides to make Peace, January 1856

Baron Peter von Meyendorff, one of the most distinguished Russian diplomats of the nineteenth century, had been ambassador in both Berlin and Vienna. He here describes the reaction of Russia's leading statesmen to the virtual ultimatum, demanding an end to the war, sent by the Austrian government to St. Petersburg on 28 December 1855.

Note by Baron P. von Meyendorff, 15 January 1856

At eight o'clock in the evening I went to the Winter Palace to take part in the committee which was to deliberate, in the presence of the Emperor, on the five propositions transmitted by Austria as a project of peace preliminaries. If this project were not accepted unreservedly Count V. Esterhazy[7] was to take his passports. The term fixed [for the Russian reply] was the 18th. The members of this committee were: Count Vorontsov, Count Orlov, Count Kisselev, Count Bludov, Prince Dolgoruky, Minister for War, the Grand Duke Constantine, Count Nesselrode and myself. The Emperor graciously took his seat and graciously indicated in a few words and in French the object of the deliberation. The Chancellor asked permission to read a memorandum in which he expressed himself in favour of acceptance pure and simple of the five points before the term had expired. He based his argument on the following considerations: The longer the war lasted the greater the number of our enemies would become, the more harsh the conditions of peace would be, as our resources must in the long run be exhausted and the future offered us no chance of success. This said, he pointed to the dangers which might result from a diplomatic rupture with Austria, to wit: a new agreement between our enemies more unfavourable than the five points, since England had been brought only with great difficulty to agree to these conditions and had reserved the right to formulate new ones if the five points were rejected by Russia. Prince [*sic*] Vorontsov spoke first, and talking in a low voice touched by emotion, but with a tone of profound conviction, said that he could not hide from himself how hard and painful a peace on the proposed bases would be, but that in thinking of the continuation of the war he saw no probability of obtaining a better one. All the probabilities on the contrary were united in favour of a peace which would be much more humiliating and which would weaken Russia for many years by imposing on her sacrifices impossible to calculate in territory, men and money; that the Crimea, the Caucasus, Finland and even Poland might

---

[7] The Austrian ambassador in St. Petersburg.

in the long run be taken from us; and that as the struggle must end at some point it was better not to wait for such a harsh extremity but to take the resolution to make peace before being forced to do so by the exhaustion of our resources and the fact that resistance was impossible.

Count Orlov applied himself above all to refuting the possible objections to peace and to showing that the criticisms of the malicious and ignorant deserved no consideration. The mass of the population, tired by the sacrifices imposed by the war, would receive with joy the news of peace. The government, better informed and alone able to take in the whole situation, should decide the question without paying attention to public outcries – which were of little importance in Russia – and for his part he was in favour of peace. Count Kisselev voted in the same sense and stressed mainly the dangers to which the continuation of the war was exposing us. Russia had conquered her new provinces only half a century ago, too short a period to make possible a complete fusion between them and the rest of the Empire – Volhynia and Podolia were already being worked on by emissaries [of Russia's enemies] and the discontented were showing themselves very active there – Finland, in spite of the goodwill its inhabitants had shown until now, was after so many sacrifices still no more than a doubtful possession ready to come once more under the sovereignty of Sweden – Poland also was so disaffected that the whole country would rise as soon as the military operations of the allies made this possible. All these countries, whose defence was uncertain in face of the numerical superiority of the enemy, might be lost, and it could not be seen how we were to reconquer them. Compared to such dangers the sacrifices which were [now] demanded of us were minimal and must be accepted rather than run such dangerous risks.

I then spoke more or less in these terms: The Chancellor's memorandum has described the political situation of Russia, Count Vorontsov has discussed the military situation and Counts Orlov and Kisselev have drawn from the internal situation arguments in favour of a prompt peace. I shall ask Your Majesty's permission to discuss the financial situation and the reasons it provides for continuing the present struggle no longer. The Minister of Finance has told Your Majesty that the continuation of the war would infallibly lead us to bankruptcy – in fact it already costs us nearly three hundred million silver roubles in extraordinary expenses, while the receipts present an enormous deficit and the productive capital of the nation is already attacked, agriculture lacks labour in more than one province and the losses the war has caused us are not even completely known. . . .

If Russia now agrees to a peace which in no way hampers the development of her resources and in no way prejudices her future, it is evident that, in a few years, with an economical system of government, she will be as strong as before the war and will then be able to accomplish things which present circumstances do not allow her to do. A peace made today may be no more than a truce; but if it were postponed for a year or two it would find the country in a state of weakness and exhaustion such that it would need fifty years to recover from it and she would be forced to observe this peace strictly by the impossibility she would find in facing a war. I vote for acceptance pure and simple and without delay of the five points. The Emperor approved of what I had said.

> O. Hoetzsch (ed.), *Peter von Meyendorff: Ein Russischer Diplomat an den Höfen von Berlin und Wien. Politischer und Privater Briefwechsel, 1826-1863* (Berlin, 1923), iii, 214-17

9   The Treaty of Paris, 30 March 1856

The provisions of this treaty can be regarded to a large extent as an effort to protect the Ottoman Empire in future against pressure from Russia, partly by its incorporation in 'the public law and system of Europe' (Article VII) and more specifically by the neutralization of the Black Sea (Articles XI and XIII). The provisions regarding the Danubian Principalities (Articles XXII-XXV) were also intended to contribute to this end. Both the neutralization of the Black Sea and the loss of part of Bessarabia (Article XX) were regarded by Russia as bitter humiliations to be undone at the first opportunity.

Article VII. Her Majesty the Queen of the United Kingdom of Great Britain and Ireland, His Majesty the Emperor of Austria, His Majesty the Emperor of the French, His Majesty the King of Prussia, His Majesty the Emperor of all the Russias, and His Majesty the King of Sardinia, declare the Sublime Porte admitted to participate in the advantages of the public law and system (*concert*) of Europe. Their Majesties engage, each on his part, to respect the independence and the territorial integrity of the Ottoman Empire; guarantee in common the strict observance of that engagement; and will, in consequence, consider any act tending to its violation as a question of general interest.

Article VIII. If there should arise between the Sublime Porte and one or more of the other signing Powers, any misunderstanding which might endanger the maintenance of their relations, the Sublime Porte, and each of such Powers, before having recourse to the use of force, shall afford the other Contracting Parties the opportunity of preventing such an extremity by means of their mediation.

Article IX. His Imperial Majesty the Sultan, having, in his constant solicitude for the welfare of his subjects, issued a firman which, while ameliorating their condition without distinction of religion or of race, records his generous intentions towards the Christian population of his Empire, and wishing to give a further proof of his sentiments in that respect, has resolved to communicate to the Contracting Parties the said firman, emanating spontaneously from his sovereign will.

The Contracting Parties recognize the high value of this communication. It is clearly understood that it cannot, in any case, give to the said Powers the right to interfere, either collectively or separately, in the relations of His Majesty the Sultan with his subjects, nor in the internal administration of his Empire.

Article X. The Convention of the 13th of July, 1841, which maintains the ancient rule of the Ottoman Empire relative to the closing of the Straits of the Bosphorus and of the Dardanelles, has been revised by common consent.

The Act concluded for that purpose, and in conformity with that principle, between the High Contracting Parties, is and remains annexed to the present Treaty, and shall have the same force and validity as if it formed an integral part thereof.

Article XI. The Black Sea is neutralized: its waters and its ports, thrown open to the mercantile marine of every nation, are formally and in perpetuity interdicted to the flag of war, either of the Powers possessing its coasts, or of any other Power, with the exceptions mentioned in Articles XIV and XIX of the present Treaty. . . .

Article XIII. The Black Sea being neutralized according to the terms of Article XI, the maintenance or establishment upon its coasts of military-maritime arsenals becomes alike unnecessary and purposeless; in consequence, His Majesty the Emperor of all the Russias, and His Imperial Majesty the Sultan engage not to establish or to maintain upon that coast any military-maritime arsenal. . . .

Article XX. In exchange for the towns, ports, and territories enumerated in Article IV of the present Treaty, and in order more fully to secure the freedom of the navigation of the Danube, His Majesty the Emperor of all the Russias consents to the rectification of his frontier in Bessarabia.

The new frontier shall begin from the Black Sea, one kilometre to the east of the Lake Bourna Sola, shall run perpendicularly to the Akerman road, shall follow that road to the *Val de Trajan*, pass to the south of Bolgrad, ascend the course of the River Yalpuck to the Height of Saratsika, and terminate at Katamori on the Pruth. Above that point the old frontier between the two Empires shall not undergo any modification.

Delegates of the Contracting Powers shall fix, in its details, the line of the new frontier. . . .

Article XXII. The Principalities of Wallachia and Moldavia shall continue to enjoy under the suzerainty of the Porte, and under the guarantee of the Contracting Powers, the privileges and immunities of which they are in possession. No exclusive protection shall be exercised over them by any of the guaranteeing Powers. There shall be no separate right of interference in their internal affairs.

Article XXIII. The Sublime Porte engages to preserve to the said Principalities an independent and national administration, as well as full liberty of worship, of legislation, of commerce, and of navigation.

The laws and statutes at present in force shall be revised. In order to establish a complete agreement in regard to such revision, a Special Commission, as to the composition of which the High Contracting Powers will come to an understanding among themselves, shall assemble, without delay, at Bucharest, together with a Commissioner of the Sublime Porte.

The business of the Commission shall be to investigate the present state of the Principalities, and to propose bases for their future organization.

Article XXIV. His Majesty the Sultan promises to convoke immediately in each of the two Provinces, a Divan *ad hoc*, composed in such a manner as to represent most closely the interests of all classes of society. These Divans shall be called upon to express the wishes of the people in regard to the definitive organization of the Principalities.

An instruction from the Congress shall regulate the relations between the Commission and these Divans.

Article XXV. Taking into consideration the opinion expressed by the two Divans, the Commission shall transmit, without delay, to the present seat of the Conferences, the result of its own labours.

The final agreement with the Suzerain Power shall be recorded in a Convention to be concluded at Paris between the High Contracting

Parties; and a hatti-sherif, in conformity with the stipulations of the Convention, shall constitute definitively the organization of those Provinces, placed thenceforward under the collective guarantee of all the signing Powers.

CONVENTION ON THE STRAITS, SIGNED BY ALL PARTIES TO THE GENERAL TREATY

Article I. His Majesty the Sultan, on the one part, declares that he is firmly resolved to maintain for the future the principle invariably established as the ancient rule of his Empire, and in virtue of which it has, at all times, been prohibited for the ships of war of foreign Powers to enter the Straits of the Dardanelles and of the Bosphorus; and that, so long as the Porte is at peace, His Majesty will admit no foreign ship of war into the said Straits.

And Their Majesties the Queen of the United Kingdom of Great Britain and Ireland, the Emperor of Austria, the Emperor of the French, the King of Prussia, the Emperor of all the Russias, and the King of Sardinia, on the other part, engage to respect this determination of the Sultan, and to conform themselves to the principle above declared. . . .

CONVENTION LIMITING NAVAL FORCE IN THE BLACK SEA, SIGNED BY RUSSIA AND THE OTTOMAN EMPIRE

Article I. The High Contracting Parties mutually engage not to have in the Black Sea any other vessels of war than those of which the number, the force, and the dimensions are hereafter stipulated.

Article II. The High Contracting Parties reserve to themselves each to maintain in that sea six steam-vessels of fifty mètres in length at the line of flotation, of a tonnage of eight hundred tons at the maximum, and four light steam or sailing vessels of a tonnage which shall not exceed two hundred tons each.

A. and P., 1856, lxi [2072], pp. 17-30

10 The Anglo-French-Austrian Treaty of 15 April 1856

This short treaty of guarantee was intended by the British and Austrian governments to buttress and supplement the Treaty of Paris (see **VI, 9** above). Its anti-Russian character is clear, though Russia is not mentioned in the text. Its effect was undermined from the start, however, by the attitude of the French government, which signed it only with reluctance.

Article I. The High Contracting Parties guarantee, jointly and severally, the independence and the integrity of the Ottoman Empire, recorded in the Treaty concluded at Paris on the 30th of March, one thousand eight hundred and fifty-six.

Article II. Any infraction of the stipulations of the said Treaty will be considered by the Powers signing the present Treaty as *casus belli.* They will come to an understanding with the Sublime Porte as to the measures which have become necessary, and will without delay determine among themselves as to the employment of their military and naval forces.

A. and P., 1856, lxi [2076], pp. 2–3

11   The Treaty of London, 13 March 1871

For fifteen years the nullification of the humiliating Black Sea clauses of the Treaty of Paris (see **VI, 9** above) had been a major political objective of Russia. The outbreak of the Franco-Prussian war allowed the Russian government to issue, on 31 October 1870, a declaration denouncing these clauses. In March 1871 a conference of the powers in London in effect accepted this declaration, since none of them was willing to oppose it. The Turks received some formal compensation in the concession to them by Article II of a very limited right to open the Straits to the warships of friendly powers.

Article I. Articles XI, XIII and XIV of the Treaty of Paris of 30 March 1856, as well as the special Convention concluded between Russia and the Sublime Porte, and annexed to the said Article XIV, are abrogated, and replaced by the following Article.

Article II. The principle of the closing of the Straits of the Dardanelles and the Bosphorus, such as it has been established by the separate Convention of 30 March 1856, is maintained, with power to His Imperial Majesty the Sultan to open the said Straits in time of peace to the vessels of war of friendly and allied Powers, in case the Sublime Porte should judge it necessary in order to secure the execution of the stipulations of the Treaty of Paris of 30 March 1856.

A. and P., 1871, lxxii [C.314], pp. 4–5

VII

THE EASTERN CRISIS OF 1875-8

1 General Fadeev on Panslav Objectives, 1869

General R. A. Fadeev was a distinguished Russian soldier and a representative of the more extreme and military aspects of the Panslav movement. The following extracts are from a contemporary English translation of his *Mnenie o vostochnom voprose*, published in December 1869, one of the most widely-read statements of the Panslav point of view. Notice his assumptions that Russia is not part of Europe and is separated from it by a natural barrier of mutual hostility, and that the smaller Slav peoples, once liberated from Turkish or German rule, must naturally and voluntarily accept Russian leadership and control. Panslav ideas were to be very influential in forming Russian public opinion during the crisis of 1875-8, though they never had much influence in the Foreign Ministry or over most Russian diplomats.

One of two courses must be adopted. Russia must either acknowledge herself to be a State in the sense of old Poland, and nothing more than a State, alien in her heart to everything outside the boundaries which have been accidentally given to her, and proceed in a decisive manner to root out every independent feature of the races of which she is composed or which are still to enter into her composition; she must in such a case sincerely and openly renounce all thought of Slavism or of the ortho-dox East, and that community with them which envenoms her rela-tions with Europe, casting them away from her and regarding them in the same manner as Prussia or France; in fact, shutting herself up at home and maintaining her borders by force, until in the course of centuries they become merged with the body of the Empire; or, leaving to the Russian people their inalienable pre-eminence in the Slavonian world, and to the Russian language its undoubted right to be the political and connecting tongue of that world, Russia must open her arms to all those who are nearer akin to her than to Europe, receiving them as younger but independent members of the same great family.

The *first* of these two decisions would be opposed to history – a dangerous road! But that is not all. Although such a decision might have been possible under the reign of Catherine II, it is at present almost impossible. We have gone too far: tribal affinities have been aroused, the Eastern Question has been raised, divided Poland has become an apple of discord between the Germanic and Russian races; the general connection of all these difficulties has visibly asserted itself, and bears a well-defined name. The relations between Russia and Europe cannot be restored to a character of sincerity until the storm has burst and been dispelled. Russia will not be believed if she does not make use of all the means at her disposal, direct and indirect, in order to solve in her own favour questions that cannot be laid aside, and which will be decided to her disadvantage if taken up by any other Power. The *first* consequence of such a course will be that the Black Sea will be entirely taken away from Russia, and that a hostile predominance will be established on it. The *second* will be the hatred of the forty millions of Slaves [*sic*] and Orthodox whom Russia will have repelled, and who will certainly in such a case join the ranks of the enemy – a course which they will not be able to avoid. The *third* will be the excessive and crushing power of the German race, neighbouring Russia. The *fourth* will be a dispute about Poland, with all its possible results; the united Germans will not voluntarily present their flank to Russia when they might protect it, nor make a present to Russia of a soil so well adapted to receive the seeds of Germanism in the future; they will not let slip an opportunity of keeping Russia constantly on the alert; they will have an account to settle with us on the shores of the Baltic. The *fifth* consequence will be 'additional articles' relative to Finland, Livonia, Bessarabia, the Crimea. By renouncing her historical destiny, Russia at the same time renounces the only allies on whom she can ever depend. We may gain a battle by our own efforts, and in our own name, but we cannot attain any objects. And at the same time we shall have to carry on a fight with the same obstacles and with the same enemies – a defensive, not an offensive struggle, not in order to terminate that struggle with a triumph, but merely to neutralize as much as possible its unfavourable issue. The historical move of Russia from the Dnieper to the Vistula, was a declaration of war to Europe, which had broken into a part of the Continent that did not belong to her. Russia now stands in the midst of the enemy's lines – such a condition is only temporary: she must either drive back the enemy or abandon her position.

But besides the two lines of action which have just been passed in review, there is a third – a middle course. This is the worst of all. It consists in irritating the whole world against us without doing anything in reality, and without making positive preparations for anything. The Lord forbid that Russia should enter upon such a course. . . .

If there be any sense in history and the liberation of the Slaves be effected, their mutual relations towards each other and towards Russia will be determined by the force of things. The independence of each member of the liberated family in his internal affairs, a separate Ruler and separate political institutions, as may be most convenient to each – all this is already settled by history. But independence in an international and military point of view is quite a different question. It is not enough to be freed, it is necessary to remain free. In the present state of Europe there is no room for a heap of small nations, disposing of their own small armies, declaring war, making peace and alliances – each in its own person. . . . The liberated East of Europe, if it be liberated at all, will require: a durable bond of union, a common head with a common council, the transaction of international affairs and the military command in the hands of that head, the Tsar of Russia, the natural Chief of all the Slaves and Orthodox. . . . Every Russian, as well as every Slave and every orthodox Christian, should desire to see chiefly the Russian reigning House cover the liberated soil of Eastern Europe with its branches, under the supremacy and lead of the Tsar of Russia, long recognized, in the expectation of the people, as the direct heir of Constantine the Great. . . . Russian affairs will be in a fair way, only when the peasant women on the banks of the Moldau or on the slopes of the Balkans shall hush their children to sleep, saying, 'Don't cry, the Russians are coming soon to help us, and they will bring you lollipops.'

General R. A. Fadeev, *Opinion on the Eastern Question* (2nd ed., London, 1876), pp. 95-7, 98-9, 100, 103

2   The Reichstadt Agreement, 8 July 1876

The revolt, stimulated by heavy taxation and agrarian grievances, which broke out in Bosnia and Herzegovina in July 1875, proved impossible for the Turkish government to suppress. Efforts by the powers to restore peace by the 'Andrassy Note' (December 1875) and the 'Berlin Memorandum' (May 1876) were unsuccessful; and by the end of June 1876 Serbia and Montenegro had gone to war with the Turks on behalf of the rebels. This forced Russia and Austria-Hungary to come to a more specific agreement than hitherto about their respective ambitions in the Balkans. A meeting of Andrassy and Gorchakov at Reichstadt in Bohemia therefore produced the important agreement of which the differing Russian and Austrian versions are given here. The really important discrepancy between the two versions is that the Austrian one rules out, in case of a Turkish defeat, the acquisition by Serbia of any territory which may threaten Dalmatia or Croatia and envisages the gain by the Habsburg Empire of almost the whole of Bosnia and Herzegovina; the Russian one however envisages the annexation by Serbia of 'some parts of Old Serbia and Bosnia' and by Montenegro of the whole of Herzegovina, thus leaving for the Habsburg Empire only part of Bosnia. The confusion on these points was later to lead to considerable tension between Russia and Austria-Hungary.

(a) *The Austrian Version*

The reasoning has been on two hypotheses: That of the Turks coming out of the struggle victorious and that of their being defeated.

In the event of the first, it was agreed not to let them obtain more than certain guarantees, which should not be excessive. Efforts were to be made to prevent the war from becoming a struggle for extermination; Serbia and Montenegro were to be maintained in the territorial limits which now circumscribe these two principalities, and the idea of a reestablishment of the Turkish fortresses in Serbia was to be opposed.

In the case of Serbia, the character of an independent state was not to be recognized; but agreement was reached to recognize it in the case of Montenegro, whatever might be the interpretation which other Powers might wish to give to give to the political position of the Black Mountain. As a consequence of this independence, the Austro-Hungarian Government has declared itself ready to close the two ports of Klek and Cattaro to all importation of arms and of munitions for the opposing parties; although it forsees very grave objections on the part of the Turkish Government to the closing of the first of these ports.

Concerning the insurgents, it was agreed (always in the event of the victory of the Turks) to make common efforts to guarantee to them the liberties and the reforms which have been requested of the Porte and promised by it.

In all the eventualities above mentioned, there was to be no question of any territorial modification, either on one side or on the other.

In passing to the second hypothesis, that of a defeat of the Turks, the following are the ideas on which agreement was reached:

Austria-Hungary having declared that she can not permit that Serbia occupy and keep by right of conquest the enclave comprised between Dalmatia, Croatia, and Slavonia, as this would mean a danger to the provinces of the Monarchy, especially to its Dalmatian littoral, which, extending like a thin ribbon, would evidently have to be annexed to the new Serbia or else place the Imperial and Royal Government under the necessity of annexing Serbia herself, which is excluded from the programme; it was agreed that Serbia should obtain an extension of territory in the Drina region in Bosnia, at the same time as in that of Novi-Bazar in Old Serbia and in the direction of the Lim. On her side Montenegro should be rounded out by the annexation of a part of Herzegovina adjoining her territories; she should obtain the port of Spizza as well as an aggrandizement in the region of the Lim, in such a way that the tongue of land which now stretches between Serbia and Montenegro should be divided between the two principalities by the course of this river.

The rest of Bosnia and Herzegovina should be annexed to Austria-Hungary. Russia should resume her natural frontiers of before 1856 and might round herself off in the region of the Black Sea and in Turkey in Asia to the extent that this should be necessary for the establishment of better frontiers for herself in this direction and to serve as an equivalent for the slice of territory to be annexed to Austria-Hungary.

Bulgaria, Rumelia, and Albania might form autonomous states. Thessaly and the island of Crete should be annexed to Greece.

Constantinople, with a territory to be determined, should become a free city.

It was equally agreed that all these ideas should be kept secret between the two Emperors and their respective Ministers; that they should not be communicated to the other Powers, and more particularly not to the Serbians and Montenegrins, until the moment of their realization should arrive.

Pribram, ii, 189–91

(b) The Russian Version

GORCHAKOV'S EXPLANATIONS	TEXT OF THE AGREEMENT
Most Secret	*It has been agreed*:
It has been judged necessary not to proclaim the principle of *absolute* non-intervention so as not to tie our hands in advance in view of certain eventualities. We insisted on the closing of the port of Klek, without which non-inter-	1. *With regard to the present*: The Powers will observe the principle of non-intervention at present, reserving the right to come to an understanding in the future if circumstances require it. The ports of Klek and Cattaro

vention would not be sincere and effective. On our side, we would not be able to regard ourselves as bound by it and, in that case, England would not observe it. Count Andrassy added to it the closure of Cattaro which has been demanded by the English so as to give this measure the character of impartiality. However the Cabinet of Vienna foresees the impossibility of preventing private help from coming to the aid of the Christians in view of the strong sympathies of the people of Dalmatia.

The Cabinet of Vienna considers this compensation as a vital condition without which she could not allow an aggrandizement of the neighbouring Slav Principalities.

If the Russian government judged it possible and useful it is reserved for it to annex the port of Batum.

shall be closed to both parties.

In no case will the Turks be helped against the Christians.

2. *With regard to the future*:

a) In case of a Turkish success the Powers shall come to an understanding to stop them if they indulge in excessive violence against the Christians.

They will demand the reestablishment of the *status quo ante* in Serbia, including the abolition of the Turkish fortresses.

As to Bosnia and Herzegovina, the Powers will insist at Constantinople that they be organized on the basis of the programme traced out by the despatch of 30 December and the Berlin Memorandum or, at least, in accordance with the Cretan settlement.

b) If the Christians are victorious: The Powers will act together to regulate the results of the war.

They will not favour the establishment of a large Slav State, but Montenegro and Serbia will be able to annex: the former Herzegovina and a port on the Adriatic, the second some parts of Old Serbia and Bosnia.

But, in such a case, Austria will have the right to annex Turkish Croatia and some parts of Bosnia contiguous to her frontiers, following a line to be agreed on.

On her side, Russia would then have the right to recover the part of Bessarabia ceded by the treaty of 1856.

If, finally, the results of a

Christian success should bring about the complete collapse of the Ottoman Empire in Europe, Bulgaria and Rumelia could form independent Principalities within their natural limits. Epirus and Thessaly would be free to join Greece.

Constantinople could be set up as a free city.

K.A., No. i (1921), 36-8

3 Gorchakov attacks the British Attitude to Russia, November 1876

This defence of Russian policy and motives by the Chancellor was in the main sincere, for Gorchakov, elderly and moderate, had no desire for territorial gains in the Balkans other than the recovery of the parts of Bessarabia lost in 1856. It must be remembered, however, that the existence of another element in Russian policy, the expansionist Panslav ambitions (see VII, 1 above) now typified above all by General N. P. Ignatiev, the Russian ambassador in Constantinople, did something to justify the often exaggerated suspicions of British public opinion. Count P. A. Shuvalov, to whom Gorchakov is here writing, was Russian ambassador in London.

Gorchakov to Shuvalov, 3 November, 1876

I see with profound surprise from your last letter that ideas of our ambitions on Constantinople and of the Testament of Peter the Great[1] continue to haunt some people in England. I confess that I thought these old wives' tales discredited and relegated with the conquest of the Indies by Russia to the realm of political mythology.

How often have the Emperors of Russia publicly repeated that no territorial annexation in Turkey enters into their policy, that they would be highly embarrassed by such an annexation and that the maintenance of the *status quo* in the East was the best of all states of affairs? Moreover, in view of our form of government, the word of our Sovereigns is not a parliamentary declaration revocable at the will of majorities. It engages their personal loyalty. How often, moreover, has it been justified

[1] The myth of a scheme of long-term Russian territorial expansion in Europe laid down by Peter I to be carried out by his successors. It originated in French propaganda at the time of the invasion of Russia by Napoleon I in 1812.

by events? If Russia had ambitions she would do what annexationist powers do, she would prepare in silence and act at the first favourable opportunity. Did she not have the chance to do this in 1829, in 1848, in 1870, when the attention and strength of Europe were absorbed elsewhere? What proof therefore must be given to the English ministry of a disinterestedness based not on political virtue but on reason and common sense? If they could forget for a moment that they are Englishmen and place themselves in the Russian position, we should ask them whether, with their hands on their hearts, they would advise the Imperial government to seek possession of Constantinople? The answer would not be in doubt. Why not credit us with as much practical sense as they have?

The only rational state of affairs for Russian interests is to leave the keys of the Black Sea in hands weak enough not to close to Russia this commercial outlet and threaten her security. Turkish domination meets these requirements. Is it our fault if the Turks have abused it, by making their domination unbearable to their Christian subjects? Has not English policy contributed to this by stirring up the distrust of the Porte for Russia through England's own rivalry with her and by helping the Porte to make force the only basis of its power?

It is really painful to see two great states which, united, could settle European questions to their mutual advantage and to the advantage of all, disturb themselves and the world by an antagonism based on prejudices or misunderstandings.

The results are palpable. English public opinion itself is stirred by them. With greater justification [so is] national and Christian sentiment in Russia, which is too close to these countries and has too many connections with them to limit itself to academic sympathies.

This imposes on the Emperor duties which His Majesty cannot disregard. But these duties are shared by the whole of civilized Europe. What prevents England from associating herself with it by joining us to protect the Christians and to share with us their gratitude and fellow-feeling? The Eastern Question is not simply a Russian question; it involves the repose of Europe, the general peace and prosperity, humanity and Christian civilization.

Is not this a field wide enough for England to place herself at the side of Russia? Have we not invited this in calling for the presence of her squadrons in the Straits? What further guarantee must be given that we have no pretension to the exclusive possession of Constantinople?

The Emperor has just spoken in this sense to Lord A. Loftus[2] with

[2] The British ambassador in St. Petersburg.

the clarity and loyalty of his Sovereign word. The English ambassador will certainly report on this.

If this assurance must be repeated, do so, my dear Count, in the most positive terms. You will be sure of interpreting faithfully the intentions of our august master.

R. W. Seton-Watson, 'Russo-British Relations during the Eastern Crisis', *Slavonic
Review*, iv (1925-6), 194-5

4 The Austro-Russian Military Convention of 15 January 1877 and Additional Convention of 18 March 1877

These agreements were the outcome of difficult negotiations which had begun in November 1876; Andrassy's claim that the Reichstadt agreement had allowed Austria-Hungary to annex all Herzegovina and nearly all of Bosnia (see **VII, 2** above) was a particular stumbling-block. On this point Gorchakov had to give way, in return merely for Austrian neutrality in a Russo-Turkish conflict. The recognition of Serbia as part of a neutral zone, which deprived Russia of freedom of action there, was also a defeat for him. The Additional Convention, though signed on 18 March, was antedated to 15 January to indicate that the two agreements were to be regarded as forming a single whole.

Article I. The High Contracting Parties, considering that the Christian and Mohammedan populations in Bosnia and in Herzegovina are too much intermingled for it to be permissible to expect from a mere autonomous organization a real amelioration of their lot, are agreed with one another to ask for these provinces in the conference of Constantinople[3] only an autonomous régime not too greatly exceeding the measure fixed by the despatch of 30 December 1875 and the guarantees of the memorandum of Berlin. As Bulgaria is placed under more favourable conditions for the exercise of autonomous institutions, they mutually engage to demand for this province in the conference a larger autonomy, buttressed by substantial guaranties.

Article II. In the case that the negotiations should not succeed, and should result in a rupture followed by war between Russia and Turkey, the Imperial and Royal Government formally pledges itself to observe

---

[3] An international conference intended to bring peace in the Balkans and introduce reforms in Turkish rule there met at Constantinople in December 1876 and January 1877 but produced no practical results.

an attitude of benevolent neutrality in the presence of the isolated action of Russia, and by its diplomatic action to paralyse, so far as this lies in its power, efforts at intervention or collective mediation which might be attempted by other Powers. ...

Article VII. His Majesty the Emperor of Austria, etc., and Apostolic King of Hungary reserves to himself the choice of the moment and of the mode of the occupation of Bosnia and of Herzegovina by his troops. It remains understood that this measure, without assuming a character of solidarity with the occupation of Bulgaria by the Russian Army, shall not present, either in its interpretation by the Government of His Imperial and Royal Majesty or in its execution, a character of hostility towards Russia. Likewise the intervention of the Russian Army in Turkey shall not present, either in its interpretation by the Imperial Government of Russia or in its execution, a character of hostility towards Austria-Hungary.

Article VIII. The High Contracting Parties reciprocally engage not to extend the radius of their respective military action:

His Majesty the Emperor of Austria, etc., and Apostolic King of Hungary, to Rumania, Serbia, Bulgaria, and Montenegro; and His Majesty the Emperor of all the Russias to Bosnia, Herzegovina, Serbia, and Montenegro. Serbia, Montenegro, and the portion of Herzegovina which separates these two principalities are to form a continuous neutral zone, which the armies of the two Empires may not cross, and intended to preserve these latter from all immediate contact. It remains understood, however, that the Imperial and Royal Government will not oppose the combined action of Serbian and Montenegrin forces outside of their own countries with the Russian troops.

Article IX. The consequences of war and the territorial modifications which would result from an eventual dissolution of the Ottoman Empire shall be regulated by a special and simultaneous convention.

ADDITIONAL CONVENTION

Article 1. The two High Contracting Parties, having as their ultimate aim the amelioration of the lot of the Christians, and wishing to eliminate any project of annexation of a magnitude that might compromise peace or the European equilibrium, which is neither in their intentions nor in the interests of the two Empires, have come to an agreement to limit their eventual annexations to the following territories:

The Emperor of Austria, etc., and King of Hungary: to Bosnia and

Herzegovina, with the exception of the portion comprised between Serbia and Montenegro, on the subject of which the two Governments reserve the right to reach an agreement when the moment for disposing of it arrives;

The Emperor of all the Russias: in Europe to the regions of Bessarabia which would reestablish the old frontiers of the Empire before 1856.

Article 2. The High Contracting Parties engage to lend each other mutual assistance in the diplomatic field, if the territorial modifications resulting from a war or from the dissolution of the Ottoman Empire should give rise to a collective deliberation of the Great Powers.

Article 3. His Majesty the Emperor of Austria, etc., and King of Hungary and His Majesty the Emperor of all the Russias, in the interview which took place between them at Reichstadt, came to an agreement in principle on the following points: In case of a territorial modification or of a dissolution of the Ottoman Empire, the establishment of a great compact Slavic or other state is excluded; in compensation, Bulgaria, Albania, and the rest of Rumelia might be constituted into independent states; Thessaly, part of Epirus, and the island of Crete might be annexed to Greece; Constantinople, with a territory of which the limit remains to be determined, might beome a free city. Their said Majesties record that they have nothing to change in these views, and declare anew that they wish to maintain them as bases of their subsequent political action.

Pribram, ii, 193-203

5 Jomini on the Russo-Turkish War of 1877-8

A. H. Jomini, the author of this letter, was a high official in the Russian Foreign Ministry; Giers, its recipient, had since December 1875 been Assistant Minister for Foreign Affairs. The letter shows well the dislike of the war with Turkey and pessimism about its outcome which reigned in Foreign Ministry circles, especially after the severe check which the Russian army had suffered before the Bulgarian fortress of Plevna from the end of July 1877 onwards. Notice also the lack of sympathy with Panslav ideals which it reveals.

A. G. Jomini to N. K. Giers, 1 September 1877

Thus we find ourselves once more faced by the dilemma of a peace more or less incomplete or a second campaign, for in the meantime the unfavourable season[4] will have come.

Which of these two alternatives shall we choose? Both of them are painful. Undoubtedly the best thing would have been, once the business had been begun, to persevere at any cost to the end. But it remains to be seen whether this is possible! I confess that according to what we hear of the privations of our soldiers, of disease, of the views of the commissariat, etc., at present the idea of going into winter quarters seems to me inadmissible. For that Rustchuk at least must be taken, and God knows whether we shall have the time. Then we must take account of the terrible expenses and finally of England and Europe.

Moreover even if, in one way or another, we finish by achieving our object, it would still be impossible for me to see things through rose-tinted glasses! In that case first of all will come the settling of accounts. Once the gunsmoke and the clouds of glory have faded away the net result will remain; that is to say enormous losses, a deplorable financial situation, and what advantages? Our Slav brothers freed, who will astonish us by their ingratitude; Austria who without striking a blow will have acquired a preponderant position; the Christian Eastern Question which will replace Turkey in the form of a duel between Greeks and Slavs, with the continuation in another form of English and western intrigues against us; finally to end the list, all the Mussulman forces henceforth concentrated in Asia Minor, that is to say an army of three to four [hundred] thousand men supported by a population fanatically opposed to us and sustained by English money and influence – lovely neighbours for the Caucasus!

This is the balance which I foresee if everything goes as well as possible. I cannot find this situation a good one, or the policy which is drawing us towards it at the cost of the country's ruin an able one! I persist in thinking that instead of pursuing these Slav chimaeras, we should have done better to see to our own Slav Christians. If the Emperor would come down from the heights and from official splendours and play the role of Haroun al Rashid, if he would visit incognito the suburbs of Bucharest and those of his own capital, he would convince himself of all there is to be done to civilize, organize and develop his own country, and he would draw the conclusion that a crusade against drunkenness and syphilis was more necessary and more profitable to Russia than the ruinous crusade against the Turks for the profit of the Bulgars!

But these ideas are too reasonable to have the least chance of success!

[4] i.e. the winter.

You will accuse me of pessimism, but I am afraid, alas! that my pessimism will be justified by the inexorable logic of events.

> C. and Barbara Jelavich (eds.) *Russia in the East, 1876-1880. The Russo-Turkish War and the Kuldja Crisis as seen through the Letters of A. G. Jomini to N. K. Giers* (Leiden, 1959), pp. 59-60

6 The Treaty of San Stefano, 3 March 1878

The fall of Plevna on 11 December 1877 allowed the Russian advance to begin once more; and on 27 January 1878 the Porte had to accept Russian terms for an armistice. The preliminary peace terms agreed on 31 January formed the basis of this treaty, which represented the fullest practical expression ever given to the Panslav ideal. Notice particularly the provision for the creation of a large autonomous Bulgaria (it was to have a coastline on the Aegean and to receive a good deal of territory to which Serbia had claims) which was to be under Russian military occupation and whose government was to be under Russian surveillance for two years. The extensive territorial gains made by Russia in Asia are also important. Montenegro, as well as being recognized as an independent state, almost trebled her territory; but Serbia gained relatively little.

Article I. To put an end to the perpetual conflicts between Turkey and Montenegro, the frontier which separates the two countries shall be rectified in conformity with the annexed map . . . in the following way. . . . [A detailed description of the frontier follows.]

A European commission, on which the Sublime Porte and the government of Montenegro shall be represented, shall be charged with fixing the definitive limits of the Principality by introducing on the spot, in the general line [of the frontier] the modifications which it shall think necessary and equitable from the point of view of the respective interests and the tranquillity of the two countries, to which it shall grant in this respect the equivalents recognized as necessary.

Article II. The Sublime Porte definitively recognizes the independence of the Principality of Montenegro. . . .

Henceforth, in case of discussion or conflict, except in the case of new territorial claims, Turkey and Montenegro shall abandon the settlement of their differences to Russia and Austria-Hungary, who shall decide them in common, as arbitrators.

Article III. Serbia is recognized as independent. . . . [A detailed description of the frontier follows.]

A Turco-Serbian commission shall establish on the spot, with the assistance of a Russian commissary, the definitive line of the frontier, within the space of three months, and shall settle definitively the questions relating to the islands of the Drina. A Bulgarian delegate shall be admitted to take part in the work of the commission when it is concerned with the frontier between Serbia and Bulgaria. . . .

Article V. The Sublime Porte recognizes the independence of Rumania, which shall establish its right to an indemnity to be discussed between the two parties.

Until the conclusion of a direct treaty between Turkey and Rumania, Rumanian subjects shall enjoy in Turkey all the rights guaranteed to subjects of the other European powers.

Article VI. Bulgaria is constituted as an autonomous and tributary principality, with a Christian government and a national militia.

The definitive frontiers of the Bulgarian principality shall be traced by a special Russo-Turkish commission before the evacuation of Rumelia by the Russian Imperial army. This commission shall take account, in working out modifications to be introduced on the spot in the general trace [of the frontier] of the principle of the nationality of the majority of the inhabitants of these areas, in conformity with the bases of peace, as well as of topographical necessities and the practical interest of the movement of the local population.

The extent of the Principality of Bulgaria is fixed, in general terms, on the annexed map, which shall serve as basis for the definitive delimitation. . . .

Article VII. The Prince of Bulgaria shall be freely elected by the population and confirmed by the Sublime Porte with the agreement of the powers. No member of the reigning dynasties of the great European powers shall be able to be elected Prince of Bulgaria.

In case the dignity of Prince of Bulgaria shall be vacant, the election of the new Prince shall take place under the same conditions and in the same form.

An assembly of Bulgarian notables, convoked at Philippopolis or Tirnovo, shall elaborate, before the election of the Prince, under the surveillance of an imperial Russian commissary and in the presence of an Ottoman commissary, the organization of the future administration in conformity with the precedents established in 1830, after the peace of Adrianople, in the Danubian principalities.

In the localities where Bulgars are mixed with Turks, Greeks, Vlachs or others, just account shall be taken of the rights and interests of these populations in the elections and the elaboration of the Organic Laws.

The introduction of the new régime in Bulgaria and the surveillance of its functioning shall be entrusted for two years to a Russian imperial commissary. At the end of the first year after the introduction of the new régime, and if agreement on this subject has been reached between Russia, the Sublime Porte and the European cabinets, they shall be able, if it is judged necessary, to add special delegates to the imperial Russian commissary.

Article VIII. The Ottoman army shall no longer remain in Bulgaria, and all the former fortifications shall be razed at the expense of the local government. . . .

Until the complete formation of a native militia sufficient for the maintenance of order, security and peace, and of which the size shall be fixed later, by an agreement between the Ottoman government and the imperial cabinet of Russia, Russian troops shall occupy the country and shall give armed support to the commissary in case of need. This occupation shall also be limited to a period of approximately two years.

The strength of the Russian corps of occupation, composed of six divisions of infantry and two of cavalry, which shall remain in Bulgaria after the evacuation of Turkey by the imperial army, shall not exceed fifty thousand men. It shall be maintained at the expense of the occupied country. The Russian occupation forces in Bulgaria shall maintain their communications with Russia not only through Rumania but also through the Black Sea ports, Varna and Burgas, where they shall be able to organize, for the duration of the occupation, the necessary facilities.

Article IX. The amount of the annual tribute which Bulgaria shall pay to the suzerain court, by depositing it in the bank which the Sublime Porte shall later designate, shall be decided by an agreement between Russia, the Ottoman government and the other cabinets at the end of the first year during which the new organization has functioned. This tribute shall be based on the average revenue of all the territory which makes up the Principality. . . .

Article XIII. All the fortresses of the Danube shall be razed. Henceforth there shall no longer be fortified places on the banks of this river, nor warships in the waters of the principalities of Rumania, Serbia and Bulgaria, apart from the normal guard-ships and light vessels intended for the policing of the river and customs work.

The rights, obligations and prerogatives of the International Commission of the Lower Danube are maintained intact. . . .

Article XIX. The war indemnities and losses imposed on Russia, which H.M. the Emperor of Russia claims and which the Sublime Porte has agreed to reimburse him, are composed of: [details follow] . . .

Total: one thousand four hundred and ten million roubles.

Taking into consideration the financial difficulties of Turkey and in agreement with the desire of H.M. the Sultan, the Emperor of Russia agrees to substitute for the payment of the greater part of the sums enumerated in the preceding paragraph the following territorial cessions:

a) The Sandjak of Toultcha, that is to say the districts (*cazas*) of Kilia, Sulina, Mahmoudié, . . . as well as the islands of the Delta and the Isle of Serpents.

Not wishing to annex this territory and the islands of the Delta, Russia reserves to herself the option of exchanging them for the part of Bessarabia detached by the treaty of 1856 and bounded on the south by the thalweg of the Kilia branch [of the Danube] and the mouth of the Stary-Stamboul. . . .

b) Ardahan, Kars, Batoum, Bayezid and the territory as far as Soganlough. . . .

The definitive limits of the territory annexed to Russia, indicated on the annexed map, shall be fixed by a commission composed of Russian and Ottoman delegates. This commission shall take account in its work of the topography of the localities and of considerations of good administration and the conditions appropriate to ensure the peace of the area.

Noradoungian, iii, 509-21

7 Salisbury on the Position in Asiatic Turkey, May 1878

Both Lord Salisbury, who had at the end of March succeeded Derby as Foreign Secretary, and Disraeli were deeply interested, for reasons of British prestige as well as of the defence of India and of the British routes to the east, in the strengthening of the Ottoman Empire in Asia and the blocking of any further Russian advance there. This letter from Salisbury to the British ambassador in Constantinople illustrates this fact, and also Salisbury's tendency to assume, perhaps unjustifiably, that the Turks could maintain their Asiatic position only with the support of one of the Great Powers. The last sentence looks forward to the British occupation of Cyprus (see **VII, 9** below).

Salisbury to Sir A. H. Layard, 9 May 1878

The great problem which the Turk will have to solve, as soon as he has got rid of the Russian army off his soil is – how to keep his Asiatic Empire together. Sooner or later the greater part of his European Empire *must* go. Bosnia and Bulgaria are as good as gone. We may with great efforts give him another lease of Thrace: and he may keep for a considerable time a hold on Macedonia and Albania and possible [*sic*] on Thessaly and Epirus. But he will not get soldiers from them: for the Mussulman population will tend more and more to recede: and it is from them alone that any effective army can be drawn. The European provinces may bring in money: and to some extent, and for some time, they may have a strategic value. But if the Turk is to maintain himself at Constantinople it is mainly with Asiatic soldiers that he will do it. The question is how is he to maintain himself in Asia. With the Russians at Kars, the idea of coming change will be rife over all Asia Minor – over Mesopotamia and Syria. If he has his own strength alone to trust to, no one will believe in his power of resistance. He has been beaten too often. The Arabs, and the Asiatics generally, will look to the Russian as the coming man. The Turk's only chance is to obtain the alliance of a great Power: and the only Power available is England.

Is it possible for England to give that alliance? I cannot speak yet with confidence: but I think so. For England the question of Turkey in Asia is very different from that of Turkey in Europe. The only change possible for the Asiatic Christians would be to come directly under the Government of Russia. There is and can be no question of autonomy – of young and struggling nationalities, and the rest of it. ... And, while Russian influence over the provinces of European Turkey would be a comparatively distant and indirect evil, her influence over Syria and Mesopotamia would be a very serious embarrassment, and would certainly through the connection of Bagdad with Bombay, make our hold on India more difficult. I do not, therefore, despair of England coming to the conclusion that she can undertake such a defensive alliance. But for that purpose it is, as I said before, absolutely and indispensably necessary that she should be nearer at hand than Malta.

British Museum, Additional MSS. 39,137, ff.
82-4

8 The Anglo-Russian Agreement of 30 May 1878

Faced by the hostility of Great Britain and Austria-Hungary, and by acute financial difficulties and an apparent threat of revolution at home, the Russian government soon realized that the San Stefano terms could not be maintained in their entirety. Early in March Gorchakov had agreed in principle with Andrassy that they should be scrutinized and approved by a congress of the powers which was to meet at Berlin. By the end of May the major points of disagreement between Great Britain and Russia, Bulgaria and the Asiatic frontier of Turkey, had been settled in essentials by an agreement embodied in three memoranda signed by Salisbury and Shuvalov, the real architects of this *détente*. Though a number of points remained unsettled the danger of an Anglo-Russian war was now at an end. Of the three memoranda the first, much the most important, is given here.

Memorandum No. 1

His Majesty the Emperor of Russia having taken note of the modifications which the Government of Her Britannic Majesty proposes to introduce into the Preliminary Treaty of San Stefano, to make it acceptable to the English Cabinet, has judged that several of them did not contradict the main purpose of the war, which was to ensure the prosperity and security of the Christian populations of the Balkan Peninsula, in guaranteeing them stable institutions and good government.

The Cabinet of St. Petersburg finds as a result that the ideas expressed by the Cabinet of St. James offer for the forthcoming Congress the bases of an entente which would have reference to the following points:

1. England rejects the longitudinal division of Bulgaria,[5] but the Representative of Russia reserves the right to put forward its advantages at the Congress, promising none the less not to insist on it against the definitive opinion of England.

2. The delimitation of Bulgaria in the south should be modified in such a way as to cut her off from the Aegean Sea in accordance with the southern delimitation of the Bulgarian provinces proposed by the Constantinople Conference. This concerns frontier questions only in so far as they refer to the exclusion of the coastline of the Aegean Sea, that is to say west of Lagos. From this point to the Black Sea coast discussion of the frontier remains open.

3. The western frontiers of Bulgaria should be rectified on the basis

---

[5] i.e. its division by a line running in a north-south and not an east-west direction.

of nationalities so as to exclude from this province non-Bulgarian populations. . . .

4. Bulgaria, reestablished within the boundaries mentioned in points 2 and 3 shall be divided into two Provinces, to wit:

One north of the Balkans should be given political autonomy under the government of a Prince, and the other, south of the Balkans, should receive an extensive administrative autonomy (for example similar to those which exist in the English Colonies), with a Christian Governor nominated with the consent of Europe for five to ten years.

5. The Emperor of Russia attaches particular importance to the withdrawal of the Turkish army from Southern Bulgaria. His Majesty would see no security or guarantee for the future of the Bulgarian population if Ottoman troops were kept there.

Lord Salisbury accepts the withdrawal of Turkish troops from Southern Bulgaria, but Russia will not object to the Congress deciding upon the way and circumstances in which Turkish troops should be allowed to enter the Southern Province to resist rebellion or invasion, actual or threatened.

However England reserves the right to insist at the Congress on the Sultan having the right to be able to quarter troops on the frontiers of the Southern Province.

The Representative of Russia reserves to himself at the Congress complete liberty in the discussion of this last proposal of Lord Salisbury.

6. The British Government asks and Russia accepts that the higher militia officers in Southern Bulgaria should be nominated by the Porte with the assent of Europe. . . .

9. As far as the war indemnity is concerned, His Majesty the Emperor has never had the intention to convert it into territorial annexations, and he does not refuse to give assurances to this effect. . . .

Without contesting the definitive decision which Russia will take on the subject of the amount of the indemnity, England reserves the right to put forward at the Congress the serious objections to it which she sees.

10. As regards the valley of Alashkert and the town of Bayezid, this valley being the great transit route for Persia and having immense value in the eyes of the Turks, His Majesty the Emperor agrees to give it back to them, but he has asked for and obtained in exchange the handing over to Persia of the small territory of Khotour, which the Commissions of the two mediating Courts have found it just to return to the Shah.

11. The Government of Her Britannic Majesty feels itself obliged to state that it would profoundly regret that Russia should insist definitively on the retrocession of Bessarabia. As it is sufficiently well established, however, that the other Signatories of the Treaty of Paris are not ready to support by arms the delimitation of Roumania stipulated in that Treaty, England does not find herself sufficiently immediately interested in this question to be justified in taking upon herself alone the responsibility of opposing the proposed change, and she thus undertakes not to challenge the definitive decision of Russia in what concerns the retrocession of Bessarabia.

In agreeing not to contest the wish of the Emperor of Russia to acquire the port of Batoum and to retain his conquests in Armenia, Her Majesty's Government does not hide the fact that it is probable that grave dangers threatening the tranquillity of the populations of Asiatic Turkey may result in future from this extension of the Russian frontier. But Her Majesty's Government is of the opinion that the duty of protecting the Ottoman Empire against this danger, which will henceforth fall in a special degree upon England, can be carried out without Europe undergoing the calamities of a new war. At the same time the Government of the Queen takes note of the assurance given by His Imperial Majesty that in future the Russian frontier in Asiatic Turkey shall not be further extended. Her Majesty's Government being as a result of the opinion that the modifications of the Treaty of San Stefano agreed to in this Memorandum are sufficient to mitigate the objections which it has to the Treaty in its present form, agrees not to oppose the Articles of the Preliminary Treaty of San Stefano which are not modified by the ten preceding points, if, after these Articles shall have been duly discussed in the Congress, Russia persists in maintaining them.

Public Record Office, F.O. 65/1022; printed in B. H. Sumner, *Russia and the Balkans, 1870-1880* (Oxford, 1937), pp. 646-8

9 The Cyprus Convention, 4 June 1878

This Anglo-Turkish agreement, consisting of a single significant article, was the outcome of the desire of Salisbury and Disraeli to have in the eastern Mediterranean a British base conveniently placed for support of the Turks in Asia against possible Russian pressure (see **VII, 7** above); Alexandretta, Crete, Lemnos and Mytilene were also discussed as candidates for this position. In fact

Cyprus never became a British base of any significance, largely because the occupation of Alexandria in 1882 gave Britain a much better one and made possession of Cyprus largely redundant from a strategic point of view.

Article I. If Batoum, Ardahan, Kars, or any of them shall be retained by Russia, and if any attempt shall be made at any future time by Russia to take possession of any further territories of His Imperial Majesty the Sultan in Asia, as fixed by the Definitive Treaty of Peace, England engages to join His Imperial Majesty the Sultan in defending them by force of arms.

In return, His Imperial Majesty the Sultan promises to England to introduce necessary reforms, to be agreed upon later between the two Powers, into the government, and for the protection, of the Christian and other subjects of the Porte in these territories; and in order to enable England to make necessary provision for executing her engagement, His Imperial Majesty the Sultan further consents to assign the Island of Cyprus to be occupied and administered by England.

> Public Record Office, F.O. 93/110/27B; printed in J. C. Hurewitz, *Diplomacy in the Near and Middle East: A Documentary Record, 1535-1914* (Princeton, 1956), i, 187-9

10 A French Comment on the Congress of Berlin

W. H. Waddington, the author of this despatch, was the chief French representative at the Berlin congress; J. A. S. Dufaure was French Prime Minister and acting Minister for Foreign Affairs. The Anglo-Russian agreement of 30 May (see above **VII, 8**) the Cyprus Convention (see above **VII, 9**) and the general agreement to Austrian occupation of Bosnia and Herzegovina (see above **VII, 4**), did much to pave the way for the success of the Congress by ensuring that solutions to many of the problems facing it had been agreed, at least in principle, before it met. Waddington correctly stresses the similarity (though by no means identity) of the British and Austrian attitudes, but also the fact that there were no real alliances between the powers taking part in the congress.

Waddington to Dufaure, 18 June 1878

From the day of their first meeting the Plenipotentiaries have not remained inactive. Several, when they arrived in Berlin to take part in such important negotiations, were entirely unknown to each other. Relations have been established, conversations have taken place. Each has tried to fathom the policies of those among whom he sought allies or suspected opponents. For my part I tried above all to understand the views of Austria-Hungary and England and to learn to what extent there was agreement between the two cabinets which, before the meeting of the Congress, opposed most directly the Treaty of San Stefano. It was no less interesting for us to see how one or the other, or both together, had since formed links with Russia on the essential questions upon which peace or war might depend.

The more or less calculated indiscretions of an English newspaper[6] had not yet thrown any light on the terms of the rapprochement brought about between the government of His Britannic Majesty and that of the Emperor Alexander, but it was already easy to see that Bulgaria had been the object of discussions and promises suitable to pave the way for a definitive entente. Without obtaining an explicit admission from Lord Beaconsfield and the Marquess of Salisbury, I have, from the first, gathered from their mouths a statement of the views of their government which conforms, in all its essentials, with the indications which today were made public. Count Andrassy, for his part, whom I saw before tackling the English plenipotentiaries, seemed to me determined to demand the setting-up of two Bulgarias, one tributary to the Porte, the other enjoying an autonomous administration but governed directly by the Sultan. Between the language of Count Andrassy and that of Lord Beaconsfield I have noticed only shades of meaning and not essential divergences which could lead to serious disagreement. Will the tributary Bulgaria, limited in the south by the Balkans, include the city of Sofia, situated in the south-west, with the adjoining territory, within her frontiers? Will the southern province, which is to be constituted under the name of Rumelia, retain Turkish garrisons or not? On these two points the Plenipotentiaries of Austria and Great Britain do not seem as yet to have taken an absolutely firm stand, but I do not see, I repeat, any reason to fear grave dissension between them when the Congress undertakes discussion of the article of the Treaty of San Stefano relating to Bulgaria.

[Britain and Austria are generally agreed on the question of Montenegro, though Britain has little direct interest in this.]

The other territorial questions, notably those of the Serbian frontiers, of the Danube delta and of Greece, have as yet been treated only incidentally in the conversations of the representatives of the powers and are also, at least in part, subordinate to the arrangements to be made for Bulgaria. I must wait until the arrangements have been definitively formulated to form a reliable judgement on the projects of

---

[6] The *Globe*, in its issue of 14 June, had published the text of the Salisbury-Shuvalov memorandum of 30 May (**VII, 8** above).

Austria on whom, in questions of this kind, the initiative naturally falls as the principal Danubian power and a neighbour of Serbia and Montenegro.

I shall confine myself at the moment to saying that the attitude of the cabinet of Vienna with regard to Bosnia becomes more and more clear-cut. In his relations with me Count Andrassy has particularly tried to stress the considerations which lead his country to seek the annexation of Bosnia; he has tried to show me that Turkey, henceforth powerless to hold this province, is obliged to seek new conditions of existence in the concentration of its strength and that thus the interests of the Porte, like those of Europe, are linked to the interest of the Austro-Hungarian monarchy. Lord Beaconsfield seemed to me not far from sharing this idea; he seems in truth to reject annexation in the strict sense; but he has no objection to an indefinite occupation which would be nothing else than disguised annexation.

I end this summary of my first impressions by a reflection which seems to me to characterize quite accurately the general state of feeling. Each power arrived here with its own ideas and, though there exist between several of them evident affinities of interest, these do not, however, show themselves on all questions. There are no groupings in the strict sense; no government here has allies with whom it is in entire and absolute agreement. Germany, whose good will towards Russia is clear, nevertheless does not defend those clauses of the Treaty of San Stefano which are directly opposed by England and Austria and which we ourselves wish to see modified. The cabinets of Vienna and London are those which must be seen as the most united. However it is not likely that the alliance of the Three Emperors will be weakened to such an extent that Austria opens her mind completely to England. At the moment Italy maintains a rather unobtrusive attitude of observation. The Turks are left in visible and probably irremediable isolation.

Documents Diplomatiques Français (1871-1914)
1st series, ii (Paris, 1930), 331-3

11   The Treaty of Berlin, 13 July 1878

This treaty, which revised that of San Stefano, marked a victory for Britain and Austria by drastically reducing in size the autonomous Bulgaria created at San Stefano. The restoration of Macedonia to Turkish rule and the creation of the new province of Eastern Rumelia, with a defensible frontier along the line of the Balkan mountains, seemed to make the Ottoman Empire in Europe once more a viable political entity. Russia for her part made appreciable territorial gains in southern Bessarabia and eastern Anatolia. Serbia and Montenegro gained relatively little by the treaty and Greece nothing; this disregard of the ambitions and claims of the small Balkan nationalities was its most fundamental defect.

Article I. Bulgaria is constituted an autonomous and tributary Principality under the suzerainty of His Imperial Majesty the Sultan; it will have a Christian Government and a national militia.

Article II. [Defines the boundaries of the principality.] This delimitation shall be fixed on the spot by the European Commission, on which the Signatory Powers shall be represented. It is understood:

    1. That this Commission will take into consideration the necessity for His Imperial Majesty the Sultan to be able to defend the Balkan frontiers of Eastern Roumelia. . . .

Article III. The Prince of Bulgaria shall be freely elected by the population and confirmed by the Sublime Porte, with the assent of the Powers. No member of the Reigning Dynasties of the Great European Powers may be elected Prince of Bulgaria.

    In case of a vacancy in the princely dignity, the election of the new Prince shall take place under the same conditions and with the same forms.

Article IV. An Assembly of Notables of Bulgaria, convoked at Tirnovo, shall, before the election of the Prince, draw up the Organic Law of the Principality.

    In the districts where Bulgarians are intermixed with Turkish, Roumanian, Greek, or other populations, the rights and interests of these populations shall be taken into consideration as regards the elections and the drawing up of the Organic Law. . . .

Article VII. The provisional *régime* shall not be prolonged beyond a period of nine months from the exchange of the ratifications of the present Treaty.

    When the Organic Law is completed the election of the Prince of Bulgaria shall be proceeded with immediately. As soon as the Prince shall have been installed, the new organization shall be put into force, and the Principality shall enter into the full enjoyment of its autonomy.
. . .

Article IX. The amount of the annual Tribute which the Principality of Bulgaria shall pay to the Suzerain Court – such amount being paid into whatever bank the Porte may hereafter designate- shall be fixed by an agreement between the Powers Signatory of the present Treaty at the close of the first year of the working of the new organization. The Tribute shall be calculated on the mean revenue of the territory of the Principality. . .

Article XIII. A province is formed south of the Balkans which will take the name of 'Eastern Roumelia', and will remain under the direct political and military authority of His Imperial Majesty the Sultan, under conditions of administrative autonomy. It shall have a Christian Governor-General.

Article XIV. [Fixes the frontiers of Eastern Roumelia.]

Article XV. His Majesty the Sultan shall have the right of providing for the defence of the land and sea frontiers of the province by erecting fortifications on these frontiers and maintaining troops there.

Internal order is maintained in Eastern Roumelia by a native gendarmerie assisted by a local militia.

In forming these corps, the officers of which are nominated by the Sultan, regard shall be paid in the different localities to the religion of the inhabitants. . . .

Article XVI. The Governor-General shall have the right of summoning the Ottoman troops in the event of the internal or external security of the province being threatened. In such an eventuality the Sublime Porte shall inform the Representatives of the Powers at Constantinople of such a decision, as well as of the exigencies which justify it.

Article XVII. The Governor-General of Eastern Roumelia shall be nominated by the Sublime Porte, with the assent of the Powers, for a term of five years.

Article XVIII. Immediately after the exchange of the ratifications of the present Treaty, a European Commission shall be formed to arrange, in concert with the Ottoman Porte, the organization of Eastern Roumelia. . . . The whole of the arrangements determined on for Eastern Roumelia shall form the subject of an Imperial Firman, which will be issued by the Sublime Porte, and which it will communicate to the Powers.

Article XXII. The strength of the Russian corps of occupation in Bulgaria and Eastern Roumelia, which shall be composed of six divisions of infantry and two divisions of cavalry, shall not exceed

fifty thousand men. . . . The period of the occupation of Eastern
Roumelia and Bulgaria by the Imperial Russian troops is fixed at nine
months from the date of the exchange of the ratifications of the present
Treaty. . . .

Article XXIII. The Sublime Porte undertakes scrupulously to apply in
the Island of Crete the Organic Law of 1868, with such modifications
as may be considered equitable.

Similar laws adapted to local requirements, excepting as regards the
exemption from taxation granted to Crete, shall also be introduced
into the other parts of Turkey in Europe for which no special organization has been provided by the present Treaty.

Article XXV. The Provinces of Bosnia and Herzegovina shall be
occupied and administered by Austria-Hungary. The Government of
Austria-Hungary, not desiring to undertake the administration of the
Sandjak of Novi-Bazar, which extends between Servia and Montene-
gro in a south-easterly direction to the other side of Mitrovitza, the
Ottoman Administration will continue to exercise its functions there.
Nevertheless, in order to assure the maintenance of the new political
state of affairs, as well as freedom and security of communications,
Austria-Hungary reserves the right of keeping garrisons and having
military and commercial roads in the whole of this part of the ancient
Vilayet of Bosnia. To this end the Governments of Austria-Hungary
and Turkey reserve to themselves to come to an understanding on the
details.

Article XXVI. The independence of Montenegro is recognized by the
Sublime Porte and by all those of the High Contracting Parties who
had not hitherto admitted it. . . .

Article XXXIV. The High Contracting Parties recognize the independence of the Principality of Servia, subject to the conditions set
forth in the following Article. [This deals with equality of civil and
political rights and freedom of worship.] . . .

Article XLIII. The High Contracting Parties recognize the independence
of Roumania, subject to the conditions set forth in the two following
Articles. . . . [The first of these deals with equality of civil and political
rights and freedom of worship.] . . .

Article XLV. The Principality of Roumania restores to His Majesty
the Emperor of Russia that portion of the Bessarabian territory de-

tached from Russia by the Treaty of Paris of 1856, bounded on the west by the mid-channel of the Pruth, and on the south by the mid-channel of the Kilia Branch and the Stary-Stamboul mouth.

Article XLVI. The islands forming the Delta of the Danube, as well as the Isle of Serpents, the Sandjak of Toultcha, . . . are added to Roumania. The Principality receives in addition the territory situated to the south of the Dobroutcha as far as a line starting from the east of Silistria and terminating on the Black Sea, south of Mangalia. . . .

Article LXVIII. The Sublime Porte cedes to the Russian Empire in Asia the territories of Ardahan, Kars, and Batoum, together with the latter port. . . .

Article LIX. His Majesty the Emperor of Russia declares that it is his intention to constitute Batoum a free port, essentially commercial.

Article LX. The valley of Alaschkerd and the town of Bayazid, ceded to Russia by Article XIX of the Treaty of San Stefano, are restored to Turkey. . . .

Article LXI. The Sublime Porte undertakes to carry out, without further delay, the improvements and reforms demanded by local requirements in the provinces inhabited by the Armenians, and to guarantee their security against the Circassians and Kurds.

   It will periodically make known the steps taken to this effect to the Powers, who will superintend their application.

                                    A. and P., 1878, lxxxiii [C.2108], pp. 15-27

VIII

THE EASTERN QUESTION, 1878-1914

1 The League of the Three Emperors, 18 June 1881

The way for this important agreement between Germany, Russia and Austria-Hungary was paved by negotiations during the winter of 1879-80 between Bismarck and Saburov, the Russian ambassador in Berlin, and by the accession to power in Great Britain, in April 1880, of the Gladstone government which was unwilling to support Austria-Hungary against Russia even to the limited extent that the Disraeli cabinet had done. In general the agreement tried to maintain in the Balkans the more or less satisfactory status quo and balance between Russian and Austrian influence established in 1878, though the protocol annexed to the treaty envisaged important territorial changes in the future. Article III was very important to Russia as giving her security against the penetration of a British fleet into the Black Sea in any future war. The treaty was renewed in 1884 but allowed to expire in 1887.

Article I. In case one of the High Contracting Parties should find itself at war with a fourth Great Power, the two others shall maintain towards it a benevolent neutrality and shall devote their efforts to the localization of the conflict.

This stipulation shall apply likewise to a war between one of the three Powers and Turkey, but only in the case where a previous agreement shall have been reached between the three Courts as to the results of this war.

In the special case where one of them should obtain a more positive support from one of its two Allies, the obligatory value of the present Article shall remain in all its force for the third.

Article II. Russia, in agreement with Germany, declares her firm resolution to respect the interests arising from the new position assured to Austria-Hungary by the Treaty of Berlin.

The three Courts, desirous of avoiding all discord between them, engage to take account of their respective interests in the Balkan Peninsula. They further promise one another that any new mod fications in the territorial status quo of Turkey in Europe can be accomplished only in virtue of a common agreement between them.

In order to facilitate the agreement contemplated by the present Article, an agreement of which it is impossible to foresee all the conditions, the three Courts from the present moment record in the Protocol annexed to this Treaty the points on which an understanding has already been established in principle.

Article III. The three Courts recognize the European and mutually obligatory character of the principle of the closing of the Straits of the Bosphorus and of the Dardanelles, founded on international law, confirmed by treaties, and summed up in the declaration of the second Plenipotentiary of Russia at the session of July 12 of the Congress of Berlin (Protocol 19).

They will take care in common that Turkey shall make no exception to this rule in favour of the interests of any Government whatsoever, by lending to warlike operations of a belligerent Power the portion of its Empire constituted by the Straits,

In case of infringement, or to prevent it if such infringement should be in prospect, the three Courts will inform Turkey that they would regard her, in that event, as putting herself in a state of war towards the injured Party, and as having deprived herself thenceforth of the benefits of the security assured to her territorial status quo by the Treaty of Berlin.

Article IV. The present Treaty shall be in force during a period of three years, dating from the day of the exchange of ratifications.

Separate Protocol of the Same Date

1. Bosnia and Herzegovina. Austria-Hungary reserves the right to annex these provinces at whatever moment she shall deem opportune.
. . .

3. Eastern Rumelia. The three powers agree in regarding the eventuality of an occupation either of Eastern Rumelia or of the Balkans as full of perils for the general peace. In case this should occur, they will employ their efforts to dissuade the Porte from such an enterprise, it being well understood that Bulgaria and Eastern Rumelia on their part are to abstain from provoking the Porte by attacks emanating from their territories against the other provinces of the Ottoman Empire.

4. Bulgaria. The three Powers will not oppose the eventual reunion of Bulgaria and Eastern Rumelia within the territorial limits assigned to them by the Treaty of Berlin, if this question should come up by the force of circumstances. They agree to dissuade the Bulgarians from all aggression against the neighbouring provinces, particularly Macedonia; and to inform them that in such a case they would be acting at their own risk and peril.

Pribram, i, 37-45

2   The Growing Crisis in Egypt

By April 1876 the extravagance of its government, heavy and improvident borrowing abroad on unfavourable terms and the greed of foreign creditors and *concessionaires*, had reduced Egypt to bankruptcy. This led to the placing of the country's finances under foreign, above all French and British, control, and a rapid growth of political discontent and nationalist feeling. By 1881 the discipline of the army was collapsing and the Khedive Tewfik had become a mere puppet in the hands of nationalist officers. The following note was therefore sent to the British and French consuls-general in Egypt for presentation to him in an effort to strengthen his position. The British government still felt strongly that any military intervention which might become necessary should be undertaken only by Egypt's Turkish suzerain; and Gladstone himself accepted with some reluctance the presentation of this note.

Anglo-French Note delivered to the Khedive on 8 January 1882

You have been instructed on several occasions to inform the Khedive and his Government of the determination of England and France to afford them support against the difficulties of various kinds which might interfere with the course of public affairs in Egypt.

The two Powers are entirely agreed on this subject, and recent circumstances, especially the meetings of the Chamber of Notables convoked by the Khedive, have given them the opportunity for a further exchange of views.

I have accordingly to instruct you to declare to the Khedive that the English and French Governments consider the maintenance of His Highness on the throne, on the terms laid down by the Sultan's Firmans, and officially recognized by the two Governments, as alone able to guarantee, for the present and future, the good order and the development of general prosperity in Egypt in which France and Great Britain are equally interested.

The two Governments being closely associated in the resolve to guard by their united efforts against all cause of complication, internal or external, which might menace the order of things established in Egypt, do not doubt that the assurance publicly given of their formal intentions in this respect will tend to avert the dangers to which the Government of the Khedive might be exposed, and which would certainly find England and France united to oppose them. They are convinced that His Highness will draw from this assurance the confidence and strength which he requires to direct the destinies of Egypt and its people.

A. and P., 1882, lxxxii [C.3106], pp. 2-3

3 The French Withdrawal from Intervention in Egypt

On 24 July the British and French governments had announced their readiness to defend the Suez Canal against the danger to which unrest in Egypt seemed to expose it; but when, five days later, Freycinet, the French Prime Minister, asked the Chamber of Deputies to vote money for an expedition with this purpose he was overwhelmingly defeated. The attitude of the deputies was strongly influenced by the fear that involvement in Egypt might divert French resources away from the overriding objective of the recovery of Alsace-Lorraine, and by the reserved and discouraging attitude to Anglo–French action taken by the German government. Great Britain now found herself, quite unexpectedly, committed to unilateral intervention in Egypt. Lord Lyons, the author of this despatch, was British ambassador in Paris; Earl Granville was Foreign Secretary.

Lord Lyons to Earl Granville, 30 July 1882

I had yesterday the honour to inform your Lordship by telegraph that the French Ministry had been defeated that afternoon on the Suez Canal Credits Bill by a very large majority.

I have the honour to transmit to your Lordship herewith the authentic account of the proceedings given in the 'Journal Officiel' this morning.

The corrected numbers of the votes differ even more than usual from those announced from the Chair by the President at the time.

The corrected numbers are:

For the Bill	75
Against it	416
Majority against the Government	341

At the beginning of the debate M. Achard stated that he should vote in favour of the Bill, on the understanding that the intervention was to be strictly confined to the protection of the Canal.

M. de Freycinet maintained that the protection of the Canal was a thing quite apart from military or political intervention in Egypt, and that there was no danger of France being led on into any further measures. He said that he had made two reservations in consenting to cooperate with England:

1. that no landing of French forces should take place on the Canal unless the navigation on it was seriously menaced to such a degree as to render a landing indispensable;

2. that the French Government would altogether refuse, in every case, to cooperate in intervention properly so called. He renewed his assurances that no action beyond these limits would be undertaken without the express consent of the Chambers, and said that the Government made a direct appeal to the confidence of the Chamber. . . .

The debate was wound up by a very remarkable speech by M. Clemenceau. He created a considerable sensation by stating that since the discussion of the Bill had been postponed two days before a double *coup de théâtre* had taken place – first, the consent of the Sultan to send troops to Egypt; and, secondly, a communication which he described in terms that plainly showed that he was acquainted with Prince Bismarck's telegram of the 27th instant.[1]

In fact, that telegram had no doubt been read by M. de Freycinet to the Committee on the Bill, of which M. Clemenceau was a member.

M. Clemenceau distinctly refused to sanction any sort of intervention, and finished his speech in the following words:

'Gentlemen, the upshot of what is now happening is this: Europe is covered with soldiers, everyone is watchful, all the Powers are reserving their freedom of action for the future; reserve France's freedom of action.'[2]

A. and P., 1882, lxxxiii [C.3391], p. 258

4 The Anglo-Turkish Convention regarding Egypt, 22 May 1887

The agreement of which the most important clauses are given here was the most serious effort made by Great Britain to withdraw from Egypt, where her position was in many ways difficult, on terms which would safeguard her

---

[1] This suggested that as the Sultan was willing to send troops to Egypt no immediate action be taken by the powers if the Turks thought they could protect the Suez Canal adequately.

[2] The quotation is in French in the original.

interests there. It was violently opposed by the French government, which disliked the postponement of the evacuation for three years and the fact that even after it had taken place Great Britain would still have a special status in Egypt. This opposition, supported at Constantinople by the Russian government, ensured that the convention was not ratified by the Porte. The British occupation thus became, unintentionally and insensibly, permanent. The provisions of Article III regarding freedom of navigation in the Suez Canal were to be reiterated in an international convention of October 1888.

Article III. The Imperial Ottoman Government will invite the Powers parties to the Treaty of Berlin to approve a Convention for better securing the freedom of navigation through the Suez Canal.

By such Convention the Imperial Ottoman Government will declare that this maritime Canal shall be always free and open, whether in time of peace or of war, for ships of war and merchant-vessels passing from one sea to the other, without distinction of flag, on payment of the dues and in conformity with the regulations actually in force, or with those which may hereafter be promulgated by the competent administration. . . .

Article IV. Inasmuch as the abnormal state of the Soudan, and the troubles caused by political events in Egypt, may for some time render necessary the adoption of ordinary precautions for the safety of the frontiers, and the internal security of Egypt, Her Britannic Majesty's Government will superintend the military defence and organization of the country.

For this purpose it will maintain in Egypt the number of British troops it may consider necessary, and will continue to exercise a general inspection of the Egyptian army. . . .

Article V. At the expiration of three years from the date of the present Convention, Her Britannic Majesty's Government will withdraw its troops from Egypt. If at that period the appearance of danger, in the interior or from without, should render necessary the adjournment of the evacuation, the British troops will withdraw from Egypt immediately after the disappearance of this danger, and two years after the aforesaid evacuation the provisions of Article IV above shall completely cease to have effect.

On the withdrawal of the British troops, Egypt shall enjoy the advantages of the principle of territorial immunity ('sûreté territoriale'), and on the ratification of the present Convention the Great Powers shall be invited to sign an Act recognizing and guaranteeing the inviolability of Egyptian territory. . . .

GPNE D

Nevertheless the Imperial Ottoman Government will make use of its right of occupying Egypt militarily if there are reasons to fear an invasion from without, or if order and security in the interior were disturbed, or if the Khediviate of Egypt refused to execute its duties towards the Sovereign Court, or its international obligations.

On its side, the Government of Her Britannic Majesty is authorized by this Convention to send, in the above-mentioned cases, troops into Egypt, which will take the measures necessary to remove these dangers. In taking these measures, the Commanders of these troops will act with all the regard due to the rights of the Sovereign Powers.

The Ottoman troops as well as the British troops will be withdrawn from Egypt as soon as the causes requiring this intervention shall have ceased.

A. and P., 1887, xcii [C.5050], pp. 52-5

5 Bismarck offers only Limited Help to Russia in Bulgaria, December 1886

In September 1885 a successful revolt broke out in Eastern Rumelia in favour of union with the principality of Bulgaria. The Russian government, reversing its attitude of 1878, opposed the union, largely because it intensely disliked the ruler of Bulgaria, Alexander of Battenberg. By September 1886 Russian pressure had forced him to abdicate, and Austro-Russian tension over the position in Bulgaria had become very acute. Bismarck, faced by a growth of anti-German feeling and aggressive nationalism in France and knowing that some Panslavs in Russia were prepared to contemplate a French alliance, now found himself in a very difficult position. As can be seen from this memorandum by a high official of the German Foreign Office, he was quite prepared to accept Russian domination of Bulgaria. But he wished above all to hold a balance between Russia and Austria-Hungary, his two allies in the League of the Three Emperors, and was quite unwilling to exert at Vienna the pressure for which the Russian government wished.

Memorandum by Count zu Rantzau, 14 December 1886

The Chancellor wishes a confidential despatch to be drafted to Herr von Schweinitz[3] covering a copy of the Russian despatch of 27 November, to the following effect:

We are ready to support the wishes of Russia, as far as possible, wherever there are effective forces at hand. But in Sofia itself we cannot go begging, unless measures of some sort, providing for the event

[3] The German ambassador in St. Petersburg.

of a refusal, have been decided upon beforehand. We are not ready to expose ourselves to the risk of expressing desires or demands to people like the Bulgarians, which they could either accept or refuse without exposing themselves to any consequences. It would be for us *une question de dignité*. We could not advance into the country, as it would be geographically impossible, and we could equally little place ourselves on an equality with the Government there. If we could threaten them in Sofia with unpleasant consequences or force as a result of a refusal, it would be a different matter; but it would be beneath our dignity to have anything to do with a request which might be rejected. . . .

[Goes on to allege at some length that at the Congress of Berlin Germany had given consistent support to all Russia's proposals and had been rewarded only with Russian hostility.]

After this experience Herr von Giers[4] cannot expect a conscientious German colleague of his own accord to break up and destroy the friendships which might be ours in case of renewed Russian disturbances in Europe; and all the less when we are already certain of the enmity of so strong a Power as France, when the fact is before us that most of the Russian Press, with the indulgence of the Imperial Government, is rousing public opinion in the country for a struggle against Germany, and when simultaneously through the French government direct disclosures of its Foreign Minister reach us to the effect that Russian overtures are being made in Paris in the sense of a joint anti-German policy.

In view of all these circumstances if Herr von Giers will be good enough to understand them, he will not be able fairly to demand of us that we go further than we have done hitherto in supporting Russia's wishes in Vienna, that is to say than energetic but friendly recommendations. Beyond this there remains only threats, which we refuse to use when dealing with Austria. In my Memorandum of 3 December I expressed my conviction that according to the spirit of existing Treaties Bulgaria should fall within the Russian sphere of influence. This opinion of ours is known in Vienna, and I am sure it does not conflict with any vital Austro-Hungarian interests. Up to September 1885, Austrian policy found this situation acceptable. The policy of His Majesty the Emperor will continue to adhere to it and as hitherto to second the Russian efforts to realize it with all diplomatic support. But I did not expect that the measure of this support would fail to satisfy M. de Giers, since he must have been informed by you of all the

4 N. K. Giers, Russian Foreign Minister 1882-94.

influence we have brought to bear in Vienna for a long time past. That he is not satisfied is clear to me from the fact that our adhesion in principle to Russia's policy in regard to Bulgaria, as shown in my Memorandum of 3 December, has had no result but a demand to increase our pressure on Austria. This, in my opinion, has already been for some time past as heavy as is possible between Powers who wish to remain friendly.

We also count on the friendship of Russia; but we have never demanded anything from her and believe that we must before all pursue a German policy and can only under certain circumstances count on benevolent passivity and diplomatic support. The latter is entirely lacking in the French question, which is the one lying nearest our heart. But so far I have never thought of expressing a wish to Herr von Giers that Russia should exercise a calming pressure on France, not in favour of any German influence outside our own frontiers, but merely to secure us against new unjust attacks like that of 1870. And even so, such Russian pressure in Paris would not be an equivalent for German pressure in Vienna, for Russia's relations with France are not strengthened by historic tradition or geographical neighbourhood. In spite of all her social relations with France, Russia has hitherto had only hostile impulses against her – in 1812, in the Crimean War of 1854 and the Polish Revolt of 1861-3; while German-Russian relations have ever since the Seven Years War remained thoroughly friendly and benevolent except for the period since 1879, directly after we had proved our good will towards Russia in the most unreserved way and without being influenced by any selfish interest in the questions that lay before us.

G.P., v, 96-100

6   The Reinsurance Treaty, 18 June 1887

Of this famous Russo-German agreement only the clauses relating to the Balkans are printed here; these were the part of the treaty which had immediate practical importance. It was Bismarck's last effort to retain some formal treaty connection with Russia after the League of the Three Emperors (**VIII, 1**) had been broken up by the Bulgarian crisis of 1886-7, and was only partly successful; Alexander III had no enthusiasm for it and the German government insisted on its being valid for a period of only three years against the five proposed by the Russians.

Article II. Germany recognizes the rights historically acquired by Russia in the Balkan Peninsula, and particularly the legitimacy of her preponderant and decisive influence in Bulgaria and in Eastern Rumelia. The two Courts engage to admit no modification of the territorial status quo of the said peninsula without a previous agreement between them, and to oppose, as occasion arises, every attempt to disturb this status quo or to modify it without their consent.

Article III. The two Courts recognize the European and mutually obligatory character of the principle of the closing of the Straits of the Bosphorus and of the Dardanelles, founded on international law, confirmed by treaties, and summed up in the declaration of the second Plenipotentiary of Russia at the session of 12 July of the Congress of Berlin (Protocol 19).

They will take care in common that Turkey shall make no exception to this rule in favour of the interests of any Government whatsoever, by lending to warlike operations of a belligerent power the portion of its Empire constituted by the Straits. In case of infringement, or to prevent it if such infringement should be in prospect, the two Courts will inform Turkey that they would regard her, in that event, as putting herself in a state of war towards the injured Party, and as depriving herself thenceforth of the benefits of the security assured to her territorial status quo by the Treaty of Berlin.

Pribram, i, 277

7   The Second Mediterranean Agreement, 12-16 December 1887

This agreement, like the Reinsurance Treaty (see **VIII, 6** above) a by-product of the Bulgarian crisis, was concluded by an exchange of notes between Great Britain, Italy and Austria of 12-16 December: the Austrian note printed below embodies its terms. The three powers had now united, with implicit German support, to prevent Russian domination of Bulgaria and perhaps even of the Ottoman Empire generally. The agreement, which supplemented and expanded one made in March 1887, was kept strictly secret at the insistence of Lord Salisbury, who feared parliamentary difficulties if it were revealed.

Count Karolyi to Lord Salisbury, 12 December 1887

Following the entente established between the Governments of His Majesty the Emperor of Austria, King of Hungary, and of their Majesties, the Queen of the United Kingdom of Great Britain and Ireland and the King of Italy, by the exchange of notes carried out in

London in the month of March 1887, the Government of His Imperial and Royal Apostolic Majesty has agreed with the Government of Italy to propose to the Government of Great Britain the adoption of the following points, intended to confirm the principles established by the aforesaid exchange of notes and to clarify the common attitude of the three Powers in anticipation of the eventualities which might arise in the East:

1. Maintenance of peace and exclusion of all agressive policies.

2. Maintenance of the status quo in the East, based on the treaties, to the exclusion of all policies of compensation.

3. Maintenance of the local autonomies established by the same treaties.

4. Independence of Turkey, guardian of important European interests (independence of the Caliphate, freedom of the Straits etc.) from all preponderant foreign influence.

5. As a result Turkey can neither cede nor delegate to another power her rights of suzerainty over Bulgaria, nor intervene to set up a foreign administration there, nor tolerate acts of coercion undertaken for this last purpose, under the form either of a military occupation or of the despatch of volunteers. In the same way Turkey, constituted by the treaties guardian of the Straits, cannot cede any part of her sovereign rights, nor delegate her authority to another Power in Asia Minor.

6. Desire of the three Powers to associate Turkey with them for the common defence of these principles.

7. In case of resistance by Turkey to illegal enterprises as they are indicated in Article 5, the three Powers will at once come to an agreement on the measures to be taken to ensure respect for the independence of the Ottoman Empire and the integrity of its territory as they are established by previous treaties.

8. If however the conduct of the Porte, in the opinion of the three Powers, should take on the character of complicity or connivance in such an illegal enterprise, the three Powers will consider themselves justified by existing treaties in proceeding jointly or separately to the provisional occupation by their land or sea forces of such places in Ottoman territory as they shall agree in recognizing it as necessary to occupy for the purpose of safeguarding the objectives laid down by previous treaties.

9. The existence and contents of the present agreement between the three Powers shall not be revealed to Turkey or to other Powers which have not already been informed of them without the previous consent of each and all of the above-mentioned three Powers.

The Undersigned Ambassador Extraordinary and Minister Pleni-potentiary of His Imperial and Royal Apostolic Majesty has been ordered by his Government to sign the present note and to exchange it for a similar note from the Government of Her Britannic Majesty.

B.D., viii, 12

8   Salisbury on the Position at the Straits, June 1892

The Russo-French alliance which began to take formal shape in August 1891 and was completed in January 1894 considerably weakened Britain's position in the Mediterranean and brought very much into question her ability to defend Constantinople and the Straits against future Russian attack. Here Salisbury outlines, somewhat pessimistically, what seemed to him some of the implications of the new position.

Memorandum by Lord Salisbury, 4 June 1892, commenting on a Joint Report by the Director of Military Intelligence and the Director of Naval Intelligence of 18 March 1892

The protection of Constantinople from Russian conquest has been the turning point of the policy of this country for at least forty years, and to a certain extent for forty years before that. It has been constantly assumed, both in England and abroad, that this protection of Con-stantinople was the special interest of Great Britain. It is our principal, if not our only, interest in the Mediterranean Sea; for if Russia were mistress of Constantinople, and of the influence which Constanti-nople possesses in the Levant, the route to India through the Suez Canal would be so much exposed as not to be available except in times of the profoundest peace. I need not dwell upon the effect which the Russian possession of Constantinople would have upon the Oriental mind, and upon our position in India, which is so largely dependent on prestige. But the matter of present importance is its effect upon the Mediterranean; and I cannot see, if Constantinople were no longer de-fensible, that any other interest in the Mediterranean is left to defend. The value of Malta, our only possession inside that sea, would at all events be diminished to an indefinite degree.

It now appears from this Report that, in the opinion of General Chapman and Captain Bridge, it is not only not possible for us to protect Constantinople, but that any effort to do so is not permissible. Even supposing the fortifications in the Dardanelles could be silenced, even supposing the Sultan asked for our presence in the Bosphorus to defend him against a Russian attack, it would yet be, in the judgement of these two officers, a step of grave peril to employ any portion of the British Mediterranean fleet in protecting him. The peril would arise, not from any danger we might incur in meeting the Russian forces, not from the strength of any fortifications the fleet would have to pass, but from the fact that this is the extreme end of the Mediterranean and that so long as the French fleet exists at Toulon, the function of the English fleet must be to remain in such a position as to prevent the French fleet at Toulon from escaping into the Atlantic and the English Channel, where it would be a grave peril to this country. They conclude, therefore, that unless we had the concurrence of France, which is of course an absurd hypothesis, or unless we had first destroyed the French fleet at Toulon, which at all events must be a very distant contingency, it is not legitimate for us to employ our fleet at the eastern end of the Mediterranean. The presence of the French fleet therefore in the harbour of Toulon, without any declaration of hostile intention or any hostile act, has the power of entirely immobilizing, and therefore neutralizing, any force that we possess or could bring under existing circumstances into the Mediterranean.

Two very grave questions arise from this strategic declaration which it must be the task of Her Majesty's Government, before any long period has elapsed, definitely to answer.

In the first place, it is a question whether any advantage arises from keeping a fleet in the Mediterranean at all. The main object of our policy is declared to be entirely out of our reach, and it is laid down that even a movement to attain it would be full of danger. There is nothing else in the Mediterranean which is worth the maintenance of so large and costly a force. If its main duty is to protect the Atlantic and the Channel, it had better go there. If it is retained in Portsmouth Harbour it will, at least, be comparatively safe from any possible attack on the part of the fleet at Toulon, and a very considerable relief will be given to the Budget of the Chancellor of the Exchequer.

Secondly, the other consideration is that our foreign policy requires to be speedily and avowedly revised. At present, it is supposed that the fall of Constantinople will be a great defeat for England. That defeat appears to be not a matter of speculation, but of absolute certainty, according to the opinion of these two distinguished officers, because we may not stir a finger to prevent it. It would surely be wise, in the interest of our own reputation, to let it be known as quickly as possible that we do not pretend to defend Constantinople, and that the protection of it from Russian attack is not, in our eyes, worthy of the sacrifices or the risks which such an effort would involve. At present, if the two officers in question are correct in their views, our policy is a policy of false pretences. If persisted in, it will involve discomfiture to all who trust in us, and infinite discredit to ourselves.

> Public Record Office, Cab 37/31/10; printed in C. J. Lowe, *The Reluctant Imperialists*: *British Foreign Policy, 1878-1902* (London, 1967), ii, 86-8

9 The Armenian Massacres, 1895-6

Tension between the Armenian minority in Asia Minor and their Turkish rulers had been growing for some time and came to a head in the form of massacres of Armenians from the early autumn of 1894 onwards. A powerful body of public opinion in Britain supported some form of action to protect the Armenians; but the disagreements of the powers, and particularly the un-cooperative attitude of the Russian government, which had Armenian subjects of its own whose nationalist claims it disliked, prevented anything effective being done. In spite of a paper scheme of reforms issued by the Porte on 20 October, the winter of 1895-6 saw worse massacres than any hitherto known. This despatch of the German Ambassador in Constantinople to the Chancellor illustrates the essentials of the diplomatic position.

Baron von Saurma to Prince von Hohenlohe, 16 December 1895

The unity which has reigned hitherto, at least on the surface, between the representatives of the Great Powers here in their dealings with the Sultan, is becoming more and more doubtful.

Sir Philip Currie[5] urges more and more that the Sultan be publicly unmasked, and the Powers thus enabled to restrain him and to prevent him from causing further mischief.

'The miscreant, who has already slaughtered nearly 100,000 people and is not yet satisfied, must finally be rendered innocuous for reasons of general humanity.'

Herr von Nelidov,[6] however, rejects all suggestions aimed at a direct attack on the Sultan and his being placed under constraint in his Government administration.

Both colleagues tried privately to win me over to their point of view. Nelidov admitted to me that his instructions positively ordered him

---

[5] The British ambassador in Constantinople.
[6] A. I. Nelidov, the Russian ambassador in Constantinople.

to support the Sultan and in all cases to refuse participation in unfriendly steps taken against him jointly by his colleagues.

Sir Philip Currie pointed to the growing dissatisfaction of public opinion in England and the resulting probability that his Government would soon be forced to act in some energetic way against the Sultan, the author of such endless human misery. Even the other Powers could not, in order to please Russia, permit the whole of Turkey to fall into complete anarchy through the guilt of Abdul Hamid.

According to instructions, I carefully kept up my reserve with both Ambassadors, and merely pointed out how desirable it appeared to me to remain united, so that through as calm and objective reports as possible to our Governments we could avoid the risk of allowing them to form divergent judgements on the situation here.

To judge by the French Ambassador's attitude, it appears that his Government – though by and large it follows Russian leadership – is not so kindly disposed towards the Sultan and his deeds as is the case in St. Petersburg, and would scarcely take Abdul Hamid's side if England one day became impatient and felt moved to more direct action.

That subtle observer, the Sultan, has long ago realized the growing change in the policy of the Powers who used to be firmly united against him, and is evidently beginning to count on Russia's support in any difficult situation he may get into.

It is clear that this will not help much to restore order in Asia Minor; but perhaps it is to the political interest also of Russia to watch conditions there become worse and worse.

In several respects the European Powers may have reason to criticize this policy; nevertheless the dangers for them arising out of conditions in Asia Minor are much more distant than those which may eventually arise from an outbreak of disorder in the European Provinces of Turkey – e.g., Macedonia.

To prevent this should now be a main objective of the 'conservative' Powers.

G.P., x, 127-8

10 A Possible Russian Seizure of the Bosphorus, December 1896

A. I. Nelidov, the Russian ambassador in Constantinople, had urged the forcible seizure of the Bosphorus by Russia in 1882, in 1892 and in the autumn of 1895. When he renewed the proposal toward the end of 1896 the apparently imminent collapse of the Ottoman Empire and the likelihood of foreign, above all British, intervention on behalf of the Armenians ensured it more serious consideration than in the past. It soon became clear that the decisions embodied in the document printed below could not be put into effect, largely because of the refusal of France, whose support was essential, to back Russian ambitions at the Straits. However it illustrates the tense and uneasy situation which prevailed in the Near East in 1895-6 and the apparent imminence of the collapse of the Ottoman Empire.

Decisions of a Conference held under the Chairmanship of His Imperial Majesty at Tsarskoe Selo, on Saturday, 5 December 1896

Those present:
    The Minister for War
    The Minister of Finance
    The Director of the Ministry of Marine
    The Chief of the General Staff
    The Director of the Ministry of Foreign Affairs
    The Russian ambassador in Constantinople

In the discussion of the memorandum drawn up by Actual Privy Councillor Nelidov on the state of affairs in the Turkish Empire and the methods to which Russia might be forced to resort in certain circumstances, State Secretary Witte expressed the opinion that the seizure of the Bosphorus, without an agreement with the other powers, at the present moment and in existing conditions was very risky and might have dangerous results.

Vice-Admiral Tyrtov then declared that it would be difficult to abandon to the Russian ambassador in Constantinople the right to summon on his own initiative the Black Sea squadron for a descent on the Bosphorus. In the opinion of the Director of the Ministry of Marine, Actual Privy Councillor Nelidov should telegraph to Sevastopol and Odessa about the prospective summons, so that the squadron could set about preparations for the descent without loss of time. These preparations would demand a certain amount of time, in view of the insufficient number of steamships available at Sevastopol at the moment, and meanwhile the order to set forth could follow from St. Petersburg without delay, on the highest authority.

It was therefore agreed by the majority of the majority of the members of the conference.

Decided:
    To empower ambassador Nelidov, on his return to his post, to in-

vestigate, together with the representatives of the other powers, in accordance with the proposal of the British government, means for the reorganization and maintenance of the Ottoman Empire on the essential condition of securing the safety of the Christian population. He should carefully avoid all methods which would lead to a gradual replacement of Turkish administration by a European one and to the establishment of an international régime on the shores of the Straits.

The ambassadors of the six great powers should do their best to achieve by discussion and exhortation the adoption of policies which appear indispensable for the achievement of the above-mentioned objective. But if the Sultan should resist the adoption of the methods proposed to him or should delay on various pretences their being put into effect, then our ambassador ought, by means of confidential talks with the representatives of the other powers, to clarify in good time exactly which method of coercion their governments think will be necessary. This method, in all probability, will be that of a naval demonstration in the Sea of Marmora, in spite of the treaty establishing the closure of the Straits. In that case, even if the Russian Mediterranean squadron took part in such a demonstration, we could not agree to the entry of a considerable number of foreign warships into the Dardanelles without subsequently occupying the Bosphorus to guarantee observance of the treaty forbidding entry into the Black Sea. Thus Actual Privy Councillor Nelidov is entrusted with the duty of warning the imperial government in advance of proposals of the other powers, so that orders can be given to the Black Sea squadron in good time, bearing in mind that from the moment of a common decision of all the powers to resort to a naval demonstration ships of their Mediterranean squadrons will need less time to enter the Dardanelles than our ships for the voyage from Sevastopol and Odessa to the Bosphorus.

As regards the present uneasy state of affairs in Turkey, it must not be lost to sight that the efforts of the ambassadors to restore peace may not avert the sudden and forcible result of the intrigues of the Armenian committees – new bloodshed and slaughter in Constantinople, or finally a general revolt against the power of the Sultan, and his overthrow. In these circumstances, the appearance of the Mediterranean squadrons before Constantinople for the protection of their subjects and the Christians might take place unexpectedly, without a preliminary agreement of the ambassadors.

In view of this, and in order not to be forestalled on the Bosphorus, the Russian ambassador is instructed, if the worst comes to the worst, to warn in advance by a secret telegram the commander-in-chief of the

Black Sea fleet of the need for the rapid despatch of a squadron for a descent on the Bosphorus, simultaneously informing the imperial government of this action.

In all events, when the Black Sea squadron sails from Sevastopol and Odessa, the ambassador is entrusted with the duty of informing the Sultan of the resulting unalterable decision [i.e. to occupy the Bosphorus] and to offer him the aid of Russia in ensuring his personal safety if he agrees to cooperate or, at least, not to oppose the entry of Russian ships into the Bosphorus and the seizure by a landing of a number of points on both shores of the Straits to guard *for ever* the entrance into the Black Sea.

K.A., Nos. 47-48 (1931), 64-7

11   The Austro-Russian Agreement on the Balkans, May 1897

This agreement, of 5 May, was the result of conversations in St. Petersburg between the Emperor Francis Joseph and the Tsar Nicholas II, with their Foreign Ministers, Count Goluchowski and Count Muraviev. In the first of the documents printed Goluchowski summarizes the result of these conversations for the Austrian ambassador in St. Petersburg; in the second the Russian government comments on the Austrian interpretation of them. The agreement did something to reduce, at least for the next six years, the intensity of the powers' involvement in the affairs of the Balkans, but clearly foreshadowed further territorial changes there.

(a) *Count Goluchowski to Prince Liechtenstein, 8 May 1897*

1. It was agreed that, in case the maintenance of the present status quo becomes impossible, Austria-Hungary and Russia discard in advance all idea of conquest in the Balkan Peninsula, and that they are decided to make this principle respected by every other Power which might manifest designs on the above-mentioned territory.

2. It was equally recognized that the question of Constantinople and of the adjacent territory as well as that of the Straits (Dardanelles and Bosphorus), having an eminently European character, is not of a nature to be made the object of a separate understanding between Austria-Hungary and Russia.

Count Mouravieff did not hesitate to declare in this connection that, far from striving for any modification of the present state of things, sanctioned by the Treaty of Paris and the Convention of London, the Imperial Government held, on the contrary, to the complete maintenance of the provisions relative thereto, which gave full and entire satisfaction to Russia in prohibiting, by the closing of the Straits, access to the Black Sea to foreign war vessels.

In its inability to admit of concession on this point, the Cabinet of St. Petersburg was only guided by a principle of legitimate security, a principle the recognition of which was accorded by us from the outset.

3. On the other hand, the establishment of a new order of things in the Balkan Peninsula, outside Constantinople and the Straits, would, in case it should occur, give rise to a special stipulation between Austria-Hungary and Russia, who, being chiefly interested in the settlement of this question, declare themselves disposed to act in common accord in fixing henceforth the bases of their understanding, to wit:

a) The territorial advantages, accorded to Austria-Hungary by the Treaty of Berlin, are and remain acquired by her. In consequence, the possession of Bosnia, of Herzegovina, and of the Sanjak of Novibazar may not be made the object of any discussion whatsoever, the Government of His Imperial and Royal Apostolic Majesty reserving to itself the right of substituting, when the moment arrives, for the present status of occupation and of right of garrisoning that of annexation.

b) The part comprised between Janina to the south and the Lake of Scutari to the north, with a sufficient extension on the east side, shall form an independent state under the name of the principality of Albania, to the exclusion of every foreign domination.

c) The rest of the territory to be disposed of shall be the object of an equitable partition between the different small existing Balkan States, a partition on the subject of which Austria-Hungary and Russia reserve the right of being heard in good time. While inclined to take into consideration as far as possible the legitimate interests of the participants, they are resolved, on the other hand, to safeguard the principle of the present equilibrium, and, if need be by means of rectifications of frontiers, to exclude every combination which would favour the establishment of a marked preponderance of any particular Balkan principality to the detriment of the others.

d) Having finally recorded that our two Cabinets have no other objective in the Balkan Peninsula than the maintenance, the consolidation, and the pacific development of the small States established there, we agreed to pursue in future in this field a policy of perfect harmony, and to avoid in consequence everything which might engender between us the elements of conflict or of mistrust.

(b) *Note of the Russian Government to Prince Liechtenstein in regard to the Balkan Agreement, 17 May 1897*

Count Goluchowski, in his note of 8 May, fixed, henceforth, as a basis of such an understanding [i.e. in case a new order of things were to be established in the Balkan Peninsula], the four following points:

a) 'The advantages accorded to Austria-Hungary by the Treaty of Berlin are and remain acquired by her.'

In subscribing to this principle, we deem it necessary to observe that the Treaty of Berlin assures to Austria-Hungary the right of military occupation of Bosnia and Herzegovina. The annexation of these two provinces would raise a more extensive question, which would require special scrutiny at the proper times and places. As to the Sanjak of Novibazar, there would also be the necessity to specify its boundaries, which, indeed, have never been sufficiently defined.

It seems to us that points *b* and *c*, having regard to the eventual formation of a principality of Albania and to the equitable partition of all the territory to be disposed of between the different small Balkan States, touch upon questions of the future which it would be premature and very difficult to decide at present.

Pribram, i, 187-91, 193

12 Brailsford on the Position in Macedonia, 1903

These comments by a British observer with considerable experience of Macedonia illustrate the difficulty of making any real improvement in the position of the Christian minorities under Turkish rule through the intervention of selfish and often disunited great powers.

It seems to me not an extravagant conclusion that the weak but irritating intervention of Europe has caused more suffering to the native Christians than it has prevented. This system is not occasional, nor is it reserved for large and grave crises. It is followed daily in the interior; and in such places as Monastir and Uskub, where few of the Powers have any subjects of their own, the consulates are maintained solely for the purpose of hearing grievances which they are impotent to redress. In some directions they succeeed. It is notorious, for example, that most if not all of the Bulgarian bishops and their lay secretaries are involved more or less directly, and more or less voluntarily, in the rebellious activities of the Macedonian Committee. The Turks know this very well, but they never dare do more than place a Bishop under a sort of courteous and temporary arrest within his own palace. In one Macedonian town I was on good terms with the Bishop, his secretary, and the Turkish prefect. The prefect one day explained to me in great detail the exact shades of revolutionary opinion which the Bishop and his secretary affected. The cleric was a Russophil and a Panslavist. The layman was an ardent Macedonian nationalist, rather distrustful of Bulgaria, and profoundly hostile to Russia. The description was good and accurate. But knowing this, and knowing the overt practices to which these opinions led, the prefect has still to receive the Bishop at his council board, and to treat him with an elaborate and ceremonial courtesy. Why? Because the Powers, and more particularly Russia, maintain him in his place, and would treat any attempt on the part of the Turkish authorities to punish or even to remove him as an occasion for serious diplomatic action. This is not a humanitarian intervention. There would have been no inhumanity in removing the Bishop. On the other hand, when the same prefect filled his noisome prison with peasant women arrested on trumped-up charges as dangerous revolutionaries, no Embassy stirred a finger to release them. This intervention is political. In effect and perhaps in intention its sole result is to weaken the Turks, to sap their self-respect, and to hasten the day when the rotting fruit will drop into the mouths of the interested Powers. I was present one day in Hilmi Pasha's audience room at Uskub, when the acting Russian consul, a member of the Embassy staff, called on political business. It was in May of 1903, three months before the general Macedonian rising. The machinery of 'reform' was in full swing. The Pasha sat among a litter of papers. His orderlies went to and fro in stockinged feet with cat-like tread carrying warrants and despatches. One heard the click of the telegraph, and felt that the bureaucratic machine was moving. The great man scribbled orders on the palm of his hand while he talked, and interrupted his conversation every few minutes to hurl some telegraphic thunderbolt. At last the Russian had his cue. He had come to protest against the wholesale arrests of suspected revolutionaries which the Pasha was carrying out all over Macedonia. It was indeed a veritable reign of terror, but indiscriminate though the arrests were, I doubt whether even a very malevolent Turk could make many mistakes. The Bulgarian movement is a national conspiracy, and it would be hard to find in all Macedonia a hundred professed Bulgarians who have not contributed willingly or otherwise to its fortunes. But the Russian would admit no such arguments. To arrest a man upon mere suspicion was illiberal. To retain him in prison without a trial was unconstitutional. To propose to banish the heads of the movement by administrative decree, as Hilmi Pasha did, was an offence against the rights of man. The Russian was a jurist of some note. His pleading was eloquent and moving, and one only wished that it could have been addressed to the ears of the late M. Plehve.[7] Hilmi Pasha was too polite or too ignorant to administer the obvious *tu quoque*. The argument was after all only a diplomatic circumlocution for something much more cogent – something about the arrears of the Russo-Turkish indemnity, or the movements of the Black Sea fleet. The result was that the suspected leaders were not banished, but released. They went back to their villages. They worked very quietly for three months, and on the appointed day Macedonia rose in arms.[8] This Russian action would have been defensible if it had been consistent. To make revolution possible by such methods would be a relatively moral policy, if one meant that it should achieve its goal of liberation. But that Russia did not intend. She used the revolution, and – at least indirectly – promoted the revolution, only in order to weaken Turkey. And that indeed has been the total effect of European intervention since the Treaty of Berlin. The Christians are not better situated but rather worse, because their oppressor is weak – and for ever reminded of his weakness, angry, suspicious, and afraid – and for ever confirmed in his suspicions. Knowing that the Turk cannot govern, Europe permits him to govern, and renders his task impossible.

> H. N. Brailsford, *Macedonia; its Races and their Future* (London, 1906), pp. 18-20

13   The Buchlau Meeting, September 1908

From the end of April 1908 A. P. Izvolskii, the Russian Foreign Minister, had made a series of approaches to the Austrian Foreign Minister, Count Aehrenthal, seeking in particular an agreement by which Austria might annex Bosnia and Herzegovina in exchange for support for the opening of the Straits to Russian warships. In mid-September the two statesmen met at Buchlau in Moravia; the Austrian version of the verbal agreement they reached is given below. The fact that nothing had been put in writing meant that almost at once acute disagreements arose over the timing of the annexation of Bosnia and Herzegovina and over whether, as a breach of the Berlin settlement of 1878

[7] V. K. von Plehve, the Russian Minister of the Interior murdered by revolutionaries in 1904, who was notorious for the severity with which he attempted to repress all revolutionary and liberal tendencies in Russia.

[8] i.e. in the revolt of August 1903.

(see **VII**, **11** above) it needed the approval at an international conference of all the signatories of that settlement.

Aehrenthal's undated Report on a Conversation with Isvolskii at Buchlau on 16 September 1908

M. Izvolskii likewise raised the question of the political consequences of the memorandum of 27 August,[9] and recognized it as being in accordance with the interests of Russia. As far as the annexation of Bosnia and Herzegovina was concerned, M. Izvolskii tried at first to entrench himself behind the Muraviev formula[10]; but when I indicated that I could not be satisfied with such an answer and that it was high time that Russia should at last take a definitive stand on this question which had been so frequently raised, he did not hesitate to tell me that Russia, if we should be forced to proceed to annexation, would assume a friendly and benevolent attitude to this event. The Russian minister at the same time recognised the great moderation and caution expressed in our renunciation of the Sandjak [of Novibazar], which gave reason to believe that the fait accompli of the annexation would most probably appear in a more favourable light because of the simultaneous withdrawal of our troops from the Sandjak.

While he was talking in general about this subject, M. Izvolskii remarked that he did not in any way regard with mistrust the consolidation of the territorial position of the [Habsburg] Monarchy which would be brought about by the annexation of Bosnia and Herzegovina. However in his consent to it he must not lose sight of the special interests of Russia, and must also weigh the results which the modification of the Treaty of Berlin brought about by us would have for the Balkan states and the general position in Turkey.

As far as Russian interests were concerned, M. Izvolskii formulated the wish which he had long cherished of a passage for Russian ships of war through the Straits. He began with a repetition of the declaration, frequently given by Russian statesmen on previous occasions, that Russia had no territorial gains in view in Constantinople or its neighbourhood. In the modification of treaty rights which he envisaged it was a matter simply of an academic definition which should offer

[9] An Austrian *aide-mémoire* of 27 August had envisaged in certain circumstances an Austrian annexation of Bosnia and Herzegovina and had offered Russia, in exchange for a friendly attitude to this, a confidential and friendly exchange of views on the question of the Straits.

[10] That 'the establishment of a new order of things in the Balkan Peninsula would, in case it should occur, give rise to a special stipulation between Austria-Hungary and Russia.' (See **VIII**, **II** above.)

Russia the possibility of strengthening her different squadrons from the reservoir of the Black Sea fleet instead of by costly shipbuilding. In this sense it would be a matter of our agreement for which he casually suggested the following wording:

'Austria-Hungary gives an undertaking to observe a benevolent and friendly attitude in the event of Russia seeing herself drawn by her interests to take steps to obtain free passage through the Dardanelles for individual Russian warships. It is understood that this modification of existing rights does not threaten the independence and security of the Ottoman capital and that the same facility cannot be refused to the other states with coastlines on the Black Sea.'

I replied to M. Izvolskii that in this connection it was a matter of preparing the ground also for a political understanding with Russia in the future. In this question we also were ready for a friendly agreement, and I could hold out the prospect of our agreement to his formula if Russia meanwhile had taken a benevolent and friendly attitude towards us at the time of the annexation of Bosnia and Herzegovina. The settlement of the question must in any event be in the sense that the passage of Russian warships should be envisaged only individually and not in squadrons, that Turkish possession of Constantinople should remain inviolate and that the security and independence of the Turkish capital should not be threatened. M. Izvolskii was greatly pleased by the prospect which I held out to him of agreement from our side to his formula, and expressed the hope that he would succeed in finding a form of words that could also be accepted by the other interested parties. To my question as to whether he had already sounded the English cabinet the Russian minister replied in the negative and remarked that the difficult task of winning over the cabinet of St. James now confronted him. Since England's interest in the question of the Straits had substantially declined in recent years, he hoped however for a favourable result in London as well. . . .

[The two statesmen then went on to agree that the proclamation of independence by Bulgaria and the union of Crete to Greece should not be regarded as making any real change in the situation in the Balkans. The Balkan states were not to be allowed to make any territorial gains at the expense of the Turks, though Serbia might be given some territory on her southern frontier if and when important changes took place in the Balkans.]

While M. Izvolskii and I discussed exhaustively the main points of the arrangement we had come to we agreed that M. Izvolskii would undertake to put on paper the main lines of the conclusions which we had reached: the Russian minister was to send me this statement as soon as possible.

On the question which M. Izvolskii finally raised, namely, when we considered the correct moment to have come for the declaration of the annexation of Bosnia and Herzegovina, I answered that it must come in the near future, as the reports from Sarajevo and Plevlje indicated. It was very easily possible that the annexation would be declared in the first days of October, immediately before the meeting of the Delegations.[11] When M. Izvolskii said that it would be preferable to him if this event took place after his return to St. Petersburg in the middle of October, since he would then be in a position to control himself the attitude of Russian public opinion, I did not hesitate to declare that it would also be much preferable to me if M. Izvolskii could be in St. Petersburg at the moment of the annexation, but that our hand was being forced by events and that I therefore, as I had said, could not guarantee that the annexation would not take place before the Delegations met; at all events he would receive from me previous warning in good time.

> *Österreich–Ungarns Aussenpolitik. Von der bosnischen Krise 1908 bis zum Kriegsausbruch 1914* (Vienna-Leipzig, 1930), i, 87-8, 90-1

14   The German Declaration to Russia, 21 March 1909

The Austrian annexation of Bosnia and Herzegovina was proclaimed early in October 1908. It aroused a storm of opposition in Serbia, which saw a large South Slav area placed more completely than ever under Habsburg rule, and in Russia, where Izvolskii's policy and the Buchlau agreement were very unpopular. For some time early in 1909 a great international war seemed possible. But the weakness of Russia and the support given by Germany to Austria-Hungary for the time being averted the danger. The despatch from the German chancellor to the German ambassador in St. Petersburg printed below, with its scarcely veiled threats, was the most important document of the crisis and forced the Russian government to give way.

Prince B. von Bülow to Count F. von Pourtalès, 21 March 1909

I request Your Excellency to tell M. Izvolsky that we learn with

---

[11] The groups of members from the Austrian and Hungarian parliaments which, under the constitutional arrangement of 1867, met to consider questions common to both halves of the Habsburg Monarchy.

satisfaction that he recognizes the friendly spirit of our proposal[12] and appears ready to fall in with it.

You will then inform M. Izvolsky that we are ready to propose to the Austro-Hungarian government that it should ask the Powers, on the basis of the Austro-Turkish agreement already communicated to them, to consent to the nullification of Article 25 of the Treaty of Berlin. But before we make a proposal of this kind to Austria-Hungary, we must know definitely that Russia will answer the Austrian note in the affirmative and declare, without any reservation, her formal agreement to the removal of Article 25. Your Excellency will therefore say to M. Izvolsky in a definite manner that we await a precise answer – yes or no; we shall have to consider any evasive, ambiguous or unclear answer as a refusal. We would then draw back and let matters take their course; the responsibility for all that happened subsequently would then fall exclusively on M. Izvolsky, after we have made a final sincere effort to be helpful to M. Izvolsky in clarifying the situation in a manner acceptable to him.

If you should find M. Izvolsky receptive, you can allow it to be seen that we will support him on an initiative emanating from him for adjusting formally the question of the recognition of Bulgaria.

You will not yourself refer to the complaints raised by M. Izvolsky against the Austrian policy towards Serbia. If this is done by the minister, I request you to remind him that even on the Russian side the Serbian reply has been recognized as unsatisfactory and that he himself has repudiated responsibility for it. In that connection recall to him the unsuitable language of the Serbian government.

In any case say to M. Izvolsky that in face of the increasingly provocative attitude of the Serbs matters press for a decision and that we therefore expect an immediate clear answer to our question.

The question of a conference has nothing to do with our *démarche*; the decision whether it is necessary or useful must be reserved, now as before, to an exchange of views among the Powers. We should have to regard its being dragged into the specific question now under discussion as an attempt at obstruction and therefore as a refusal of our proposal.

G.P., xxvi Pt.2, 693-5

[12] A suggestion made by Bülow on 14 March that the powers should recognize the Austrian annexation of Bosnia snd Herzegovina by an exchange of notes with Austria; this would mean the abandonment by Russia of the demand she had hitherto been putting forward for an international conference on the matter.

IX

EUROPEAN ECONOMIC ACTIVITY IN THE OTTOMAN EMPIRE IN THE LATER NINETEENTH AND EARLY TWENTIETH CENTURIES

1 Concession for the Construction of the Suez Canal, 5 January 1856

Ferdinand de Lesseps, a former French consul who had served in Egypt and had considerable influence there, obtained on 30 November 1854, from the Khedive Said, the first concession for the cutting of a canal through the Suez isthmus. It was replaced in January 1856 by this more detailed and important one, though it was not until 1858 that de Lesseps was able to float in Paris his *Compagnie Universelle du Canal Maritime de Suez*.

Second Act of Concession and Specification for the Construction and Management of the Great Maritime Suez Canal and Supplementary Works, 5 January 1856

I OBLIGATIONS

Article I. The Society founded by our friend M. Ferdinand de Lesseps, in virtue of our grant of the 30th of November 1854, must execute at its own expense, risk and peril, all works and constructions necessary for the establishment.

First. A Canal for the navigation of large vessels, between Suez on the Red Sea, and the gulf of Pelusium in the Mediterranean.

Second. A Canal of irrigation, for the navigation of the Nile, joining the river to the Maritime Canal above-mentioned.

Third. Two branches for irrigation and alimentation derived from the preceding Canal and bearing their waters in the two directions of Suez and of Pelusium.

The works to be conducted in such a manner as to be finished in six years' time, except in the case of unavoidable hindrances and delays.

Article II. The Company are to have all facilities for executing the works with which it [*sic*] is charged, by itself and with administrative powers (*in régie*), or to cause them to be executed by contractors by means of adjudication or otherwise. In all cases four-fifths at least of the workmen employed in these works are to be Egyptians. . . .

II   CONCESSIONS

Article X. In return for the construction of the Canals and the additional works mentioned in the foregoing articles, the Egyptian Government allows the Company, without tax or duty, to enjoy the use of all land not belonging to private individuals which they may require. . . .

Article XII. The Egyptian Government will make over, if occasion arise, to the Company, any private property the possession of which may be necessary to the execution of the work and the administration of the grants, provided the Company pay a just indemnity to the owners. . . .

Article XIII. The Egyptian Government invests the privileged Company, for the whole term of the grant, with power to work any mines and quarries that are public property free of duty, tax, or indemnity, and extract all materials necessary for the purposes of constructing and maintaining the works and establishments belonging to the undertaking.

It frees the Company, moreover, from all Custom-house dues, of export or import, on the importation into Egypt of all merchandise and materials whatsoever from abroad for the needs of the Company's different works in course of construction or management.

Article XIV. We declare solemnly, for ourselves and our successors, subject to the ratification of H.I.M. the Sultan, the Great Maritime Canal of Suez to Pelusium and the ports belonging to it, open at all times, as neutral passages, to every merchant vessel crossing from one sea to the other, without any distinction, exclusion, or preference of persons or nationalities, in consideration of the payment of the dues, and the performance of regulations established by the universal privileged Company for the use of the said Canal and its dependencies.

Article XV. In consequence of the principle laid down in the foregoing article, the universal privileged Company cannot, in any case, give to any vessel, Company, or private individual, any advantage or favour not given to all other vessels, Companies, or individuals, on the same conditions.

Article XVI. The duration of the Company is fixed at 99 years, counting from the completion of the works and the opening of the Maritime Canal to large vessels. . . .

Article XVIII. . . . since grants of land and other advantages have been bestowed upon the Company by the foregoing Articles, we reserve, for the benefit of the Egyptian Government, a deduction of 15 per cent upon the net profits of each year settled and allotted by the general meeting of shareholders.

P. H. Fitzgerald, *The Great Canal at Suez*
(London, 1876), i, 297-305

2 The British Purchase of Shares in the Suez Canal, November 1875

The British government had at first opposed the building of the canal as tending to strengthen France's position in the Near East; but from the moment of its opening to traffic in November 1869 the large majority of the ships passing through it were British. This stimulated a desire in London to acquire at least a share in the ownership of the canal; and in November 1875 the desperate financial plight of the Khedive Ismail offered a means of achieving this. The danger that his shares might fall into the hands of a French syndicate dictated the haste with which the transaction was completed, with the help of a loan from the Rothschild banking firm.

Treasury Minute, 25 November 1875

The First Lord and the Chancellor of the Exchequer state to the Board, that Her Majesty's Government have received a telegram from Her Majesty's Consul-General in Egypt, to the effect that the Khedive has offered to sell his shares in the Suez Canal to Her Majesty for the sum of 100,000,000 fr., and that His Highness will pay interest at the rate of 5 per cent upon the amount paid upon the shares until the coupons are free, His Highness having disposed of his interest in the coupons for some time to come.

The First Lord and the Chancellor further state that they have been in communication with Messrs N. de Rothschild and Sons, who, in the event of the offer being accepted, are prepared to carry out the operation as the agents of Her Majesty's Government in London; with that object Messrs Rothschild will undertake to hold 1,000,000*l* sterling at the disposal of the Egyptian Government, on the 1st of December next, as soon as they receive an assurance from Her Majesty's Government that the shares in question have been handed over to Her Majesty's Consul-General in Egypt. They will provide the remaining 3,000,000*l* sterling in the months of December and January, and hold them at the disposal of the Khedive in such manner as may be arranged between His Highness and themselves.

Messrs Rothschild will charge a commission of 2½ per cent upon the 4,000,000*l* sterling which they thus undertake to provide, and they will receive the 5 per cent interest which the Khedive undertakes to pay upon the amounts advanced, from the date of the advance thereof, until the date of repayment by Her Majesty's Government.

The First Lord and the Chancellor inform the Board that these several proposals have been considered and accepted by Her Majesty's Advisers, and that they have telegraphed to Her Majesty's Consul-General in Egypt that they agree to purchase the shares, 177,642 in number,[1] held by the Khedive, for the sum of 4,000,000*l* sterling, and that the money will be provided in the manner proposed by Messrs Rothschild.

The First Lord and the Chancellor point out that Messrs Rothschild undertake this heavy liability on the pledge of Her Majesty's Government that they will submit the engagement for the sanction of Parliament, and endeavour to obtain the necessary powers to enable them to repay the advance, and pay Messrs Rothschild's commission, as soon as may be practicable after the meeting of Parliament; and they recommend that a letter embodying that pledge in an official form should be written to Messrs Rothschild without delay.

My Lords approve.

Write to Messrs Rothschild.

A. and P., 1876, lxxxiii [C.1391], p.5

3   The Baghdad Railway Concession, 5 March 1903

A German syndicate had been granted a concession for the building of a railway

[1] There were in fact only 176,602, since the others had been sold some years earlier. The purchase price was adjusted accordingly.

from Constantinople to Ankara in October 1888; and other German interests
were given a concession for the construction of a line from Koniah to Baghdad
and eventually to the Persian Gulf in December 1899. The definitive concession
for the Baghdad Railway is, however, the one given below. The Ottoman
Anatolian Railroad Company, to which the concession was granted, was con-
trolled mainly by the *Deutsche Bank* and a number of French investors; and
efforts by it to raise capital in Great Britain to enable it to take advantage of this
concession were unsuccessful. The Baghdad Railway scheme helped for the
next decade to strain Russo-German and Anglo-German relations in the Near
East.

Article I. The Imperial Ottoman Government grant the concession for
the construction and working of an extension of the line from Konia
to Baghdad and Busra, passing through, or as near as possible to, the
towns of Karaman, Eregli, Kardash-Beli, Adana, Hamidieh, Osmanieh,
Bagtcheh, Kazanali, Killis, Tel-Habesh, Harran, Ras-ul-Ain, Nisibin,
Avniat, Mosul, Tekrit, Sadidjeh, Baghdad, Kerbela, Nedjef, Zobeir,
and Busra, as well as the following branches:

  1. From Tel-Habesh to Aleppo.
  2. From a neighbouring point on the main line, to be agreed upon,
to Urfa.

The Imperial Ottoman Government will not grant a guarantee,
under any form, for the construction of this branch line, about 30 kms
in length, nor any appropriation for working expenses, but the gross
receipts of every description from the branch line shall belong exclusively to the concessionaires.

  3. From Sadidjeh to Khanikin.
  4. From Zobeir to a point on the Persian Gulf to be agreed upon
between the Imperial Ottoman Government and the concessionaires,
as well as everything appertaining to the said lines. The main line and
its branches shall follow a route to be approved by the Imperial
Ottoman Government – to the Ottoman Anatolian Railway Company on the following conditions:

Article II. The duration of this concession shall be ninety-nine years. A
similar period shall be adopted for the lines of Angora and Konia, and
shall commence to run from the date of issue of the firman and the
exchange of the present convention.

As regards the new lines, this period of ninety-nine years shall
commence to run separately for each section from the date on which
the Imperial Government shall have issued the Government bonds to
the concessionnaires in accordance with Article xxxv of the present
convention. . . .

Article IV. The concessionnaires undertake to commence work on the first section, at their own expense, risk, and peril, within three months from the date of approval of the plans and designs of those first 200 kms and likewise to complete it not later than two years from that same date.

The concessionnaires undertake to commence work within three months from the date of approval of the plans and designs of the other sections, and to complete the whole of the lines and branches within eight years from the date of the issue of the firman and the exchange of the present convention. Notwithstanding, any period of delay . . . in the issue of the bonds by the Imperial Government to the concessionnaires, shall be added to the said period of eight years. . . .

Article VI. The enterprise being of public utility, land necessary for the building of the railway and everything appertaining thereto, quarries, and gravel-pits for ballast necessary for the railway and belonging to private persons, shall be taken over in accordance with the law on expropriation, whenever it has not proved possible to come to an understanding between the concessionnaires and the owners for the purchase of such land.

The Government shall expropriate and hand over to the concessionnaires land necessary for the building of the line and everything appertaining thereto after the location of the railway has been approved and staked out. The land shall be handed over by the Government within two months. . . .

Article VIII. Manufactured material for the permanent way and the materials, iron, wood, coal, engines, carriages and waggons, and other stores necessary for the initial establishment as well as the general enlargement and development of the railway and everything appertaining thereto which the concessionnaires shall purchase in the Empire or import from abroad shall be exempt from all inland taxes and customs duties. The exemption from customs duties shall also be granted for the coal necessary for working the line which is imported from abroad by the concessionnaires until the gross receipts of the line and its branches reach 15,500 fr. per kilometre. . . .

Article X. The wood and timber necessary for the construction and working of the railway may be cut in the forests of the neighbouring districts which belong to the State, in accordance with the regulations relating thereto. . . .

Article XXII. The concessionnaires may work any mines which they shall discover within a zone of 20 kms each side of the middle of the line, provided that they conform with the laws and regulations relating thereto, but this shall not give them a privilege or monopoly. . . .

Article XXIII. The concessionnaires shall have the right to build at their own expense at Baghdad, Busra, and at the terminus of the branch from Zobeir, harbours with all necessary arrangements for bringing ships alongside the quay and for the loading, unloading, and warehousing of goods. . . .

Article XXXV. The Imperial Government guarantee to the concessionnaires an annuity of 11,000 fr. per kilometre constructed and worked, and also a contract sum of 4,500 fr. per annum for working expenses in respect of each kilometre worked. . . .

If the gross kilometric receipts of the line exceed 4,500 fr. but do not exceed 10,000 fr., the surplus above 4,500 fr. shall belong entirely to the Government.

If the gross kilometric receipts exceed 10,000 fr., the portion up to 10,000 fr. being always divided as stated above, 60 per cent of the surplus over and above the 10,000 fr. shall pass to the Imperial Government, and 40 per cent to the Company.

It is agreed that if the gross kilometric receipts do not reach 4,500 fr. the sum required to make good the deficiency in this amount shall be paid to the concessionnaires by the Government at the same time as the annuity of 11,000 fr. from the special assignments to be agreed on between the Imperial Government and the concessionnaires before the fulfilment by the concessionnaires of the clauses of the present convention relative to each section. . . .

Article XXXVII. The concessionnaires undertake to carry out at their own expense all the improvements on the old lines from Haidar-Pasha to Angora and Eskishehr to Konia required for the introduction of an express train service, but the expenditure involved shall not exceed a sum of 8,000,000 fr.

In return for this expenditure and for the new extraordinary charges for working expenses involved in the introduction of the express train service, the Imperial Government assign to the concessionnaires –

1. An annuity of 350,000 fr. for thirty years for interest and sinking fund in respect of the capital sum of 8,000,000 fr. mentioned above.

This annuity shall be paid from the commencement of the works of improvement.

2. An annuity of 350,000 fr. for the establishment of the express trains.

This latter annuity shall not become payable till the main line reaches Aleppo.

A. and P., 1911, ciii [Cd. 5635], pp. 37-46

4 The Anglo-German Convention regarding the Baghdad Railway, 15 June 1914

By an Anglo-Turkish agreement of July 1913 the Turkish government recognized the autonomy of the sheikhdom of Kuweit. Strengthened by this, and by other agreements which provided that British goods carried on the Baghdad Railway should not be discriminated against and that British navigation rights on the Tigris and Euphrates should be respected, the British government was able by the convention given here to abandon its opposition to the building of the railway. Note the important proviso that the line was to terminate at Basra and not to reach the Persian Gulf proper. The outbreak of the First World War a few weeks later meant that this convention never came into effect.

Article 1. Clause (a) Recognizing the general importance of the completion of the Baghdad Railway for international commerce, His Britannic Majesty's Government undertake not to take or encourage any measures likely to impede the construction or management by the Baghdad Railway Company of the Baghdad Railway system or to prevent the participation of capital in this undertaking.

Clause (b) The Imperial German Government declare that they will use their best endeavours to secure that two British members, agreeable to His Britannic Majesty's Government, shall be admitted as representatives of British shareholders to the Board (Conseil d'Administration) of the Baghdad Railway Company.

Article 2. Clause (a) The Baghdad Railway Company having concluded with the Imperial Ottoman Government an arrangement on the following basis, the Imperial German Government and His Britannic Majesty's Government declare, so far as concerns themselves, that they adhere to the said arrangement, and will use their best endeavours to secure its due execution:

(i) The terminus of the Baghdad Railway Company's line shall be at Basra, and the Baghdad Railway Company has renounced all claims to construct a branch line from Basra (Zobeir) to the Persian Gulf referred to in Article 1 of the Baghdad Railway Convention of the 5th March, 1903, and to build a port or railway terminus on the Persian Gulf, under Article 23 of the said Baghdad Railway Convention. . . .

(v) The construction and exploitation of the proposed ports of Basra and Baghdad, authorized by Article 23 of the Baghdad Railway Convention of the 5th March, 1903, shall be carried out by a separate Ottoman Company. . . .

Clause (b) The Imperial German Government declare that they will not oppose the acquisition by British interests of 40 per cent of the share-capital of the separate Ottoman Company for the construction and exploitation of the ports of Basra and Baghdad, mentioned in sub-clause (v) above, and their rateable representation on the Board (Conseil d'Administration) of the port company, and in the contracts, if any, for construction and maintenance.

Article 3 Clause (a) The Imperial German Government and His Britannic Majesty's Government declare that they will in no case support the construction of a branch from Basra (Zobeir) or from any point of the main line of the Baghdad Railway, to the Persian Gulf unless and until there is complete agreement on the subject between the Imperial Ottoman Government, the Imperial German Government, and His Britannic Majesty's Government.

Clause (b) The Imperial German Government declare that they will in no case themselves establish, or support any claim by any persons or corporations whatsoever to establish, a port or railway terminus on the Persian Gulf unless and until there is complete agreement on the subject between the Imperial German Government and His Britannic Majesty's Government.

Clause (c) His Britannic Majesty's Government declare that they will in no case themselves establish, or support any claim by any persons or corporations whatsoever to establish, in Ottoman territory, railway undertakings either in direct competition with the Baghdad Railway Company's lines, or in contradiction with that company's existing rights, unless and until there is complete agreement on the subject between the Imperial German Government and His Brittanic Majesty's Government. For the purposes of this article, the western terminus of the Baghdad Railway system shall be held to be at Konia and the eastern terminus at Basra.

B.D., x Pt.II, 398-408

X

THE GROWTH OF NATIONALISM IN THE NEAR EAST IN THE EARLY TWENTIETH CENTURY

1 Programme of the League of the Arab Fatherland, 1905

Arab nationalism developed slowly from the 1860s onwards, above all in Syria, where it was fed by western intellectual and educational influences. The foundation in Paris in 1905 of the League of the Arab Fatherland marks an important stage in this development; its programme, of which an extract is given here, was the first significant explicit demand for separation of the Arab provinces from the Ottoman Empire and their achievement of independence and unity. The separation of civil and religious authority which it envisaged, though foreshadowed in various ways by the reforms of the Tanzimat period, none the less marked a radical break with Islamic tradition.

Nothing is more liberal than the league's programme: the Arab Fatherland. The league wants, before all else, to separate the civil and the religious power, in the interest of Islam and the Arab nation, and to form an Arab empire stretching from the Tigris and the Euphrates to the Suez Isthmus, and from the Mediterranean to the Sea of Oman. The form of government will be a constitutional sultanate based on the freedom of all religions and the equality of all citizens before the law. It will respect the interests of Europe, all the concessions and all the privileges which have been granted to her up to now by the Turks. It will also respect the autonomy of the Lebanon, and the independence of all the principalities of Yemen, Nejd, and Iraq. The league offers the throne of the Arab Empire to that prince of the Khedivial family of Egypt who will openly declare himself in its favour and who will expend his energy and his resources to this end. It rejects the idea of

unifying Egypt and the Arab Empire under the same monarchy, because the Egyptians do not belong to the Arab race; they are of the
African Berber family and the language which they spoke before
Islam had no resemblance to Arabic. There exists, moreover, between
Egypt and the Arab Empire a natural frontier which must be respected
on pain of introducing into the new state the germs of discord and
destruction. Never, moreover, did the ancient Arab caliphs succeed for
any length of time in controlling the two countries at the same time.

The Arab Fatherland also offers the universal religious caliphate over
the whole of Islam to that sherif[1] who will sincerely embrace its cause
and devote himself to this work. The religious caliph will have as a
completely independent political state the whole of the present vilayet
of the Hedjaz, with the town and the territory of Medina, as far as
Akaba. He will enjoy sovereign honours and will hold a real moral
authority over all the Musulmans of the world. One of the principal
causes of the fall of the vast empire of the Arabs was the centralization
in a single hand of civil and religious power. It is also for this reason
that the caliphate of Islam has become today so ridiculous and so contemptible in the hands of the Turks. The successor of the Prophet of
Allah must enjoy an incontestable moral prestige; his whole life must
be of unblemished honour, his authority without diminution, his
majesty independent. Thus his power will be universal; from his
residence he will rule morally over all the Musulmans of the universe
who will hurry in pilgrimage to the sanctuaries of Mohammed.

> Negib Azoury, *Le Réveil de la Nation Arabe
> dans l'Asie Turque* (Paris, 1905), pp. 245-7

2   A British Comment on the Young Turk Revolution of 1908

The revolt which overthrew the despotism of Abdul Hamid II in July 1908 was
essentially a military movement. It was inspired by resentment of the Sultan's
stifling rule, by fears of further foreign interference in the Ottoman Empire and
further losses of territory to foreign powers, and by discontent over arrears of
army pay. Here the British ambassador gives a short official report on the
revolution and its somewhat mixed reception.

*Extract from Annual Report for Turkey for the Year 1908, enclosed in Sir
G. Lowther to Sir Edward Grey, 22 February 1909*

For some years past, in and out of Turkey, it was generally known that

---

[1] i.e. descendant of the Prophet Mohammed.

a revolutionary movement set on foot by Young Turks was proceeding, but it was also generally thought that, thanks to the very complete system of espionage established by the Sultan, the development of the idea was surrounded by almost insuperable difficulties. Everyone's action in Turkey was watched, every tongue was gagged. The leader of the movement, Murad Bey (at one time its most active member) was cajoled back to Yildiz,[2] and this seemed to be a check to it, for Paris was the headquarters of the movement. Exiles for the cause there were in different parts of the Empire and in different parts of Europe, and under these circumstances it seemed that the movement could not have much cohesion . . .

[The Report goes on to describe the beginnings of the revolt in Macedonia and its progress, culminating in the demand for the re-establishment of the constitution of 1876.]

A Council of Ministers was called on the 23rd July. There were but two alternatives – to surrender to the demand, or to fight the rebels. It must have indeed appeared incomprehensible to His Majesty that, with the immense army he had always maintained, a handful of rebels could not be suppressed. But the Ministers realized that things had gone too far to turn back, and on the suggestion of Said Pasha they declared that their advice to the Sultan must be to grant the Constitution. The decision was communicated to His Majesty. The scene that followed and the circumstances under which His Majesty decided to agree to it will perhaps never become public property. Nor is it possible to say whether His Majesty, in granting the Constitution, hoped that circumstances might play into his hands and enable him to withdraw it again, or whether the report that the 2nd and 3rd Army Corps would immediately march on Yildiz if he did not agree, exercised an influence over His Majesty.

All we know is that Said Pasha left the room with instructions to take the necessary measures and to declare that His Majesty had consented to renew the ill-fated Contitution of 1876, and on the 24th July an Imperial Iradé was sent to the Governors of provinces instructing them to hold the necessary elections for the Chamber of Deputies, in accordance with the Constitution of 1876. Liberty of the press was immediately granted, and in the early days articles of praise were showered on the Sultan for his wisdom and graciousness in granting the Constitution. The spies, who had permeated every corner, disappeared as the snow before the sun, and the enthusiasm of the people, of all races and creeds,

[2] The imperial residence in Constantinople.

knew no bounds. Determination of all to combine in working for the good of the Empire and loyalty to the Sultan formed the keynote of the early days of the revolution. A general amnesty was declared for all political exiles and refugees. As a result of the sinking of all differences at that moment, it may be recorded that, on the suggestion of the Mutessarif, the President of the Bulgarian Committee and the Greek Archbishop at Serrcs met in a fraternal embrace. . . .

Englishmen were the recipients of many expressions of friendliness from Turks, who felt that the new movement could rely upon our moral support. There was a general feeling that the new reform had a better chance of success than all the reforms granted by Abdul Hamid in the past. It had not been brought about by direct foreign pressure upon the Sultan, nor was it the work of a few statesmen ahead of their time like the promulgation of the Constitution of 1876. It had been obtained by the joint pressure of the army and His Majesty's Mussulman subjects, and the almost immediate cessation of band activity[3] gave hopes that the reform would benefit Moslems and Christians alike. . . .

[The Report goes on to describe the consolidation of the new régime and its reception abroad.]

In the meantime the idea of the Constitution was being gradually assimilated throughout the country. Amongst the Arabs it produced little impression, they seemed sceptical of reform, tolerating Turkish rule as a Moslem rule, and harbouring some veneration for the Sultan as the religious head of the Ottoman Empire. There were whispers of reaction, but in most cases it could be explained by the hesitation of those, who were not convinced of the future success of the movement, declining to throw themselves into the movement with enthusiasm. The Committee of the League,[4] which showed remarkable evidence of organization, considering they had until July been working in the dark, occupied themselves by sending emissaries into the provinces to explain the nature of the movement, the programme they had for the future, and in some cases, establishing an organisation for securing the election of their candidates at the forthcoming elections. . . .

[The Report goes on to describe a growth of hostility to the new régime from the autumn of 1908.]

There were certain factors at work directed against the tendencies of

---

[3] i.e. the activities of rival armed bands of Christians and Muslims, and of Christians of different nationalities, above all in Macedonia.

[4] The Society of Union and Progress, the most important revolutionary organization in the empire.

GPNE F

reform. The stubborn and unyielding principle of the Moslem religion, which though perhaps less hasty, is more fixed and unrelenting in Turkey than in any other Mahomedan country.

The idea of equality with Christians was abhorrent to them, and there were strong evidences in the provinces that these Moslem tendencies were coming to the fore. The crowd of dismissed officials seemed inclined to join these ranks. The numerous strikes had unsettled the working classes, who were prepared to present fresh demands. . . . Moreover the attitude of the Sultan appeared to be ambiguous, and the feast of Ramazan appeared to offer every prospect of trouble between the strict Moslems and the adherents of the new régime and of liberal ideas. Fears of massacres in Anatolia were almost universal, but nothing occurred.

B.D., v, 249-59

3   Resolutions of the Arab-Syrian Congress at Paris, 21 June 1913

It will be seen that this congress (whose members came in fact almost entirely from Syria) asked only for reform, decentralization and linguistic concessions; the demand for complete independence of the Arab provinces, put forward in 1905 (**X**, 1 above) was still uttered only by a small number of expatriate intellectuals. However the idea of Arab independence was slowly growing; in 1911 a secret society was formed in Paris to work for it.

1. Radical and urgent reforms are necessary in the Ottoman Empire.

2. It is important to guarantee the Ottoman Arabs the exercise of their political rights by making effective their participation in the central administration of the Empire.

3. It is important to establish in each of the Syrian and Arab vilayets a decentralized régime appropriate to their needs and aptitudes. . . .

5. The Arabic language must be recognized in the Ottoman Parliament and considered as an official language in the Syrian and Arab provinces.

6. Military service shall be regional in the Syrian and Arab vilayets, except in case of extreme necessity. . . .

8. The Congress affirms its sympathy for the reformist and decentralizing demands of the Armenian Ottomans.

9. The present resolutions shall be communicated to the Ottoman Imperial Government.

10. These resolutions shall also be communicated to the powers friendly to the Ottoman Empire.

B.D., x Pt.II, p. 826

4 Arab Nationalist Manifesto disseminated from Cairo at the beginning of the First World War

This manifesto is interesting in its combination of an appeal to ancestral traditions with denunciations of 'economic imperialism' and an insistence on the essentially linguistic character of Arab nationalism and its ability to rise above traditional religious antagonisms. The violence of its language foreshadows many later Arab pronouncements of this kind.

Announcement to the Arabs, Sons of Qahtan

O Sons of Qahtan! O Descendants of Adnan![5] Are you asleep? And how long will you remain asleep? How can you remain deep in your slumber when the voices of the nations around you have deafened everyone? Do you not hear the commotion all around you? Do you not know that you live in a period when he who sleeps dies, and he who dies is gone forever? When will you open your eyes and see the glitter of the bayonets directed at you, and the lightning of the swords which are drawn over your heads? When will you realize the truth? When will you know that your country has been sold to the foreigner? See how your natural resources have been alienated from you and have come into the possession of England, France and Germany. Have you no right to these resources? You have become humiliated slaves in the hands of the usurping tyrant; the foreigner unjustly dispossesses you of the fruit of your work and labour and leaves you to suffer the pangs of hunger. How long will it be before you understand that you have become a plaything in the hand of him who has no religion but to kill the Arabs and forcibly to seize their possessions? The Country is yours, and they say that rule belongs to the people, but those who exercise rule over you in the name of the Constitution do not consider you part of the people, for they inflict on you all sorts of suffering, tyranny, and persecution. How, then, can they concede to you any political rights? In their eyes you are but a flock of sheep whose wool is to be clipped, whose milk is to be drunk, and whose meat is to be

[5] Qahtan and Adnan were legendary ancestors of the Arabs.

eaten. Your country they consider a plantation which they inherited from their fathers, a country the inhabitants of which are their humble slaves. Where is your Qahtanic honour? Where your Adnanian pride?

The Armenians, small as their numbers are when compared to yours, have won their administrative autonomy in spite of the opposition of the Turkish state, 'and they will presently become independent. Their people will then become self-governing, free and advanced, free and active in the social organization of humanity, in contrast to you, who will remain ever enslaved to the descendants of Genghis and Hulagu, who brought to an end your advanced Arab government in Baghdad, the Abode of Peace; and to the descendants of Tamerlane who built a tower composed of the heads of eighty thousand Arabs in Aleppo. Till when will you go on acquiescing in this utter humiliation, when your honour is made free of, your wives raped, your children orphaned . . . your money taken to be spent in the palaces of Constantinople, full as they are with intoxicating drink, musical instruments, and all kinds of wealth and luxury, and your young men driven to fight your Arab brethren, sometimes in the Yemen, sometimes in Kerek, sometimes in the Hauran, thus reinforcing the persecutions of the Turks while you remain silent and accept this monstrous imposition? Why do you shed your blood at the behest of the Turk in fighting your brethren, while you refuse it for the safeguard of your rights and the honour of your race, as the Armenians have done and are still doing? . . . Has your Arab blood become congealed in your veins, and has it changed into dirty water? You have become, by God, . . . a subject of mockery and derision among the peoples. You have become almost proverbial in your humility, weakness, and acquiescence in great loss. . . .

And O ye Christian and Jewish Arabs, combine with your brethren the Muslim Arabs, and do not follow in the footsteps of him who says to you, whether he be one of you or not: The Arab Muslims are sunk in religious fanaticism, therefore we prefer the irreligious Turks. This is nonsensical speech which proceeds from an ignorant man who knows neither his own nor his people's interest. The Muslim Arabs are your brethren in patriotism, and if you find among them some who are seized with an ugly fanaticism, so likewise are such to be found among you. Both sides, indeed, have learned it from the non-Arabs. Our ancestors were not fanatical in this sense, for Jews and Christians

---

[6] A reform of 8 February 1914, inspired mainly by Russian pressure, created two largely Armenian provinces in eastern Anatolia with a foreign inspector-general as the supreme civil authority in each.

used to study in the Mosques of Baghdad and the Andalus like brethren. Let them, both sides, aim at tolerance and at the removal of these ugly fanaticisms. For you must know that those who do not speak your tongue are more harmful to you than the ignorant fanatics among the Arabs who are your brethren in patriotism and race, while it is difficult for you to reach agreement with these contemptible creatures who are at the same time your enemies and the enemies of the Muslim Arabs. ...

Know, all ye Arabs, that a *fada'i* society has been formed which will kill all those who fight the Arabs and oppose the reform of Arab lands. The reform of which we speak is not on the principle of decentralization coupled with allegiance to the minions of Constantinople, but on the principle of complete independence and the formation of a decentralized Arab state which will revive our ancient glories and rule the country on autonomous lines, according to the needs of each province. This state will begin by liquidating some flattering foxes among the Arabs who are, and have always been, the means whereby these murderous minions have trampled on our rights, as the world will see when they proceed to bring about the disasters they have in store for us.

Sylvia G. Haim, *Arab Nationalism: An Anthology* (Berkeley-Los Angeles, 1962), pp. 83-8

5 The Deportation and Massacre of Armenians in 1915-16

In a few months in 1915-16 perhaps 800,000 Armenians in eastern Anatolia perished as a result of mass deportations carried out by the Turkish authorities. How far these deportations, and the resulting deaths by hunger, disease and massacre, were premeditated, and how far, as the Turkish government argued, a measure necessary for the safety of the Ottoman Empire because of Armenian sympathies with the Russian armies in the Caucasus and the danger of an Armenian revolt, is still debated. They greatly weakened what hope there was of the resurrection of an independent Armenian state.

Baibourt: Narrative of an Armenian Lady deported in the Third Convoy; Communicated by the American Committee for Armenian and Syrian Relief

The Armenian population of Baibourt was sent off in three batches; I was among the third batch. My husband died eight years ago, leaving me and my eight-year-old daughter and my mother a large property, so that we were living in comfort. Since mobilization began, the

Ottoman Commandant has been living in my house free of rent. He told me not to go, but I felt I must share the fate of my people. I took three horses with me, loaded with provisions. My daughter had some five-lira pieces round her neck, and I carried some twenty liras and four diamond rings on my person. All else that we had was left behind. Our party left on the 14th June, fifteen gendarmes going with us. The party numbered four or five hundred persons. We had got only two hours away from home when bands of villagers and brigands in large numbers, with rifles, guns, axes, etc., surrounded us on the road, and robbed us of all we had. The gendarmes took my three horses and sold them to Turkish mouhadjirs, pocketing the money. They took my money and the gold pieces from my daughter's neck, also all our food. After this they separated the men, one by one, and shot them all within six or seven days – every male above fifteen years old. By my side were killed two priests, one of them over ninety years of age. The brigands took all the good-looking women and girls and carried them off on their horses. Very many women and girls were thus carried off to the mountains, among them my sister, whose one-year-old baby they threw away; a Turk picked it up and carried it off, I know not where. My mother walked till she could walk no further, and dropped by the roadside on a mountain top. We found on the road many of those who had been deported from Baibourt in the previous convoys; some women were among the killed, with their husbands and sons. We also came across some old people and little infants still alive but in a pitiful condition, having shouted their voices away. We were not allowed to sleep at night in the villages, but lay down outside. Under cover of the night indescribable deeds were committed by the gendarmes, brigands and villagers. Many of us died from hunger and strokes of apoplexy. Others were left by the roadside, too feeble to go on.

One morning we saw fifty or sixty wagons with about thirty Turkish widows, whose husbands had been killed in the war; and these were going to Constantinople. One of these women made a sign to one of the gendarmes to kill a certain Armenian whom she pointed out. The gendarmes asked her if she did not wish to kill him herself, at which she said 'Why not?' and, drawing a revolver from her pocket, shot him dead.

The Treatment of Armenians in the Ottoman Empire: Documents Presented to Viscount Grey of Fallodon, Secretary of State for Foreign Affairs (London, 1916), pp. 242-3

XI

THE FIRST WORLD WAR AND
THE PEACE SETTLEMENT, 1914-23

1 The Turco-German Treaty of Alliance, 2 August 1914

German influences, above all in military affairs, had been growing in Constantinople for some time before 1914. Overtures for an alliance between the two states were first made on 22 July by a group of Turkish statesmen headed by Enver Pasha, the War Minister: they were inspired by a belief that the Ottoman Empire must, in self-defence, be associated with one of the two great-power groupings in Europe. The German government at first showed little enthusiasm for the proposal, and the alliance was a hastily-arranged and unplanned affair.

1. The two Contracting Powers undertake to observe strict neutrality in the present conflict between Austria-Hungary and Serbia.

2. In the event that Russia should intervene with active military measures and thus should create for Germany a casus foederis with respect to Austria-Hungary, this casus foederis would also come into force for Turkey.

3. In the event of war, Germany will leave its Military Mission at the disposal of Turkey.

The latter, for its part, assures the said Military Mission an effective influence over the general conduct of the army, in conformity with what has been agreed upon directly by His Excellency the Minister of War and His Excellency the Chief of the Military Mission.

4. Germany obligates itself, by force of arms if need be, [to defend] Ottoman territory in case it should be threatened. . . .

8. The present treaty shall remain secret and may be made public only following agreement between the two High Contracting Parties.

Die Deutschen Dokumente zum Kriegsausbruch
(Charlottenburg, 1919), iii, 183-4

2 The Anglo-Franco-Russian Agreements of March-April 1915

The Russian initiative of 4 March, from which these agreements sprang, was stimulated by the obvious imminence of an Anglo-French attack on the Dardanelles and fear in St. Petersburg of resulting British or French dominance of the Straits area. British acquiescence to Russia's demands was fairly readily forthcoming, though in return substantial compensations were demanded, as seen in (c) below. That of France was slower ((d) below) and given only after Russia had agreed in negotiations of 15-17 March to the creation of a French sphere of influence in Syria and Cilicia. Russia now seemed in a position, if the allies won the war, to realize age-old dreams of an annexation of Constantinople and the Straits.

(a) *Russian Circular Telegram of 4 March 1915*

The course of recent events leads His Majesty Emperor Nicholas to think that the question of Constantinople and the Straits must be definitively solved, according to the time-honoured aspirations of Russia.

Every solution will be inadequate and precarious if the city of Constantinople, the western bank of the Bosphorus, of the Sea of Marmara and of the Dardanelles, as well as southern Thrace to the Enos-Midia line, should not henceforth be incorporated into the Russian Empire.

Similarly, and by strategic necessity, that part of the Asiatic shore that lies between the Bosphorus, the river Sakharia and a point to be determined on the Gulf of Ismid, and the islands of the Sea of Marmara, the islands of Imbros and Tenedos, must be incorporated into the [Russian] Empire.

The special interests of France and of Great Britain in the region designated above will be scrupulously respected.

The Imperial Government entertains the hope that the above considerations will be sympathetically received by the two allied Governments. The said allied Governments are assured similar understanding on the part of the Imperial Government for the realization of plans which they may form in other regions of the Ottoman Empire or elsewhere.

(b) *British aide-Mémoire to the Russian Government, 12 March 1915*

Subject to the war being carried on and brought to a successful conclusion, and to the desiderata of Great Britain and France in the Ottoman Empire and elsewhere being realized, as indicated in the

Russian communication herein referred to, His Majesty's Government will agree to the Russian Government's *aide-mémoire* relative to Contantinople and the Straits, the text of which was communicated to His Britannic Majesty's Ambassador by his Excellency M. Sazonof on 4 March instant.

(c) *British Memorandum to the Russian Government, 12 March 1915*

... From the British *aide-mémoire* it follows that the desiderata of His Majesty's Government, however important they may be to British interests in other parts of the world, will contain no condition which could impair Russia's control over the territories described in the Russian *aide-mémoire* of 4 March, 1915.

In view of the fact that Constantinople will always remain a trade *entrepôt* for South-Eastern Europe and Asia Minor, His Majesty's Government will ask that Russia shall, when she comes into possession of it, arrange for a free port for goods in transit to and from non-Russian territory. His Majesty's Government will also ask that there shall be commercial freedom for merchant-ships passing through the Straits, as M. Sazonof has already promised. ...

Sir E. Grey points out that it will obviously be necessary to take into consideration the whole question of the future interests of France and Great Britain in what is now Asiatic Turkey; and, in formulating the desiderata of His Majesty's Government with regard to the Ottoman Empire, he must consult the French as well as the Russian Government. As soon, however, as it becomes known that Russia is to have Constantinople at the conclusion of the war, Sir E. Grey will wish to state that throughout the negotiations, His Majesty's Government have stipulated that the Mussulman Holy Places and Arabia shall under all circumstances remain under independent Mussulman dominion.

Sir E. Grey is as yet unable to make any definite proposal on any point of the British desiderata; but one of the points of the latter will be the revision of the Persian portion of the Anglo-Russian Agreement of 1907 so as to recognise the present neutral sphere as a British sphere. ...

(d) *Note Verbale communicated by M. Paléologue to M. Sazonov, 18 April 1915*

The Government of the [French] Republic will give its agreement to the Russian *aide-mémoire* addressed by M. Isvolsky to M. Delcassé on 6 March last, relating to Constantinople and the Straits, on condition that war shall be prosecuted until victory and that France and Great

Britain realise their plans in the East as elsewhere, as it is stated in the Russian *aide-mémoire*

B.D.F.P., 1st series, iv, 635-8

3   The Treaty of London, 26 April 1915

This treaty between Italy, Great Britain and France ended a process of bargaining over Italy's entry into the war on the side of the Entente powers which had been in progress for months. The heavy bribe offered to her for her support included, in addition to a promise of the Trentino, Istria and a large part of Dalmatia, the concessions in the eastern Mediterranean and Asia Minor given below. These were likely to introduce a further element of complication into the post-war position in the Near East, particularly as they would almost certainly conflict with the ambitions of Greece in Asia Minor.

Article 8. Italy shall receive entire sovereignty over the Dodecanese Islands which she is at present occupying.

Article 9. Generally speaking, France, Great Britain and Russia recognize that Italy is interested in the maintenance of the balance of power in the Mediterranean and that, in the event of the total or partial partition of Turkey in Asia, she ought to obtain a just share of the Mediterranean region adjacent to the province of Adalia, where Italy has already acquired rights and interests which formed the subject of an Italo-British convention. The zone which shall eventually be allotted to Italy shall be delimited, at the proper time, due account being taken of the existing interests of France and Great Britain.

The interests of Italy shall also be taken into consideration in the event of the territorial integrity of the Turkish Empire being maintained and of alterations being made in the zones of interest of the Powers.

If France, Great Britain and Russia occupy any territories in Turkey in Asia during the course of the war, the Mediterranean region bordering on the Province of Adalia within the limits indicated above shall be reserved to Italy, who shall be entitled to occupy it.

A. and P., 1920, li [Cmd. 671], pp. 5-6

4   The MacMahon Promises to the Sherif Husein, 24 October 1915

The Sherif Husein of Mecca had approached the British for support against the

Turks (essentially to strengthen the position of his own family in the Hejaz) as early as February 1914. Negotiations between him and Sir Henry MacMahon, the British High Commissioner in Egypt, went on from July 1915 to February 1916. In this letter MacMahon promised British support for Arab independence in Arabia, Syria and Irak, subject to the reservations stated with regard to the western areas of Syria, the vilayets of Baghdad and Basra, and French interests in general. The fact that the southern frontier of Syria was not defined in the letter allowed the British government later to argue, not altogether convincingly, that Palestine was not included in the area covered by MacMahon's promise.

Sir Henry MacMahon to the Sherif Husein, 24 October 1915

. . . It is with great pleasure that I communicate to you on their behalf [i.e. that of the British Government] the following statement, which I am confident you will receive with satisfaction:

The two districts of Mersina and Alexandretta and portions of Syria lying to the west of the districts of Damascus, Homs, Hama and Aleppo cannot be said to be purely Arab, and should be excluded from the limits demanded [i.e. those of the area of Arab independence.]

With the above modification, and without prejudice to our existing treaties with Arab chiefs, we accept those limits.

As for those regions lying within those frontiers wherein Great Britain is free to act without detriment to the interests of her ally, France, I am empowered in the name of the Government of Great Britain to give the following assurances and make the following reply to your letter:

1. Subject to the above modifications, Great Britain is prepared to recognize and support the independence of the Arabs in all the regions within the limits demanded by the Sherif of Mecca.

2. Great Britain will guarantee the Holy Places against all external aggression and will recognize their inviolability.

3. When the situation admits, Great Britain will give to the Arabs her advice and will assist them to establish what may appear to be the most suitable forms of government in those various territories.

4. On the other hand, it is understood that the Arabs have decided to seek the advice and guidance of Great Britain only, and that such European advisers and officials as may be required for the formation of a sound form of administration will be British.

5. With regard to the *vilayets* of Baghdad and Basra, the Arabs will recognise that the established position and interests of Great Britain necessitate special administrative arrangements in order to secure these

territories from foreign aggression, to promote the welfare of the local populations and to safeguard our mutual economic interests.

A. and P., 1938-9, xxvii [Cmd.5957], p. 8

5   The Sykes-Picot Agreement, 26 April-23 October 1916

This series of agreements grew out of negotiations which began in November 1915 between Georges Picot, former French Consul-General in Beyrut, and Sir Mark Sykes, the Assistant Secretary to the British War Cabinet. By an agreement reached on 3 January 1916 Britain was to control Mesopotamia as far north as Baghdad, and the ports of Haifa and Acre, with a sphere of influence linking these two areas. France was to control the coastal areas of Syria and the whole of Cilicia, with a sphere of influence running eastwards to the Persian frontier. Palestine was to come under some form of international régime. Difficult Franco-Russian negotiations during the next four months led to some modification of the French sphere of influence and gave Russia, by an agreement of 26 April, large territorial gains in Armenia and Kurdistan. The documents quoted below outline, in their final form, the gains to be made by the three allied powers.

(a) *Sir Edward Grey to M. Cambon, 16 May 1916*

I have the honour to acknowledge the receipt of your Excellency's note of the 9th instant, stating that the French Government accept the limits of a future Arab State, or Confederation of States, and of those parts of Syria where French interests predominate, together with certain conditions attached thereto, such as they result from recent discussions in London and Petrograd on the subject.

I have the honour to inform your Excellency in reply that the acceptance of the whole project, as it now stands, will involve the abdication of considerable British interests, but, since His Majesty's Government recognize the advantage to the general cause of the Allies entailed in producing a more favourable internal political situation in Turkey, they are ready to accept the arrangement now arrived at, provided that the cooperation of the Arabs is secured, and that the Arabs fulfil the conditions and obtain the towns of Homs, Hama, Damascus and Aleppo.

It is accordingly understood between the French and British Governments:

1. That France and Great Britain are prepared to recognize and protect an independent Arab State or a Confederation of Arab States

in the areas (A) and (B) marked on the annexed map, under the suzerainty of an Arab chief. That in area (A) France, and in area (B) Great Britain, shall have priority of right of enterprise and local loans. That in area (A) France, and in area (B) Great Britain, shall alone supply advisers or foreign functionaries at the request of the Arab State or Confederation of Arab States.

2. That in the blue area France, and in the red area Great Britain, shall be allowed to establish such direct or indirect administration or control as they may desire and as they may think fit to arrange with the Arab State or Confederation of Arab States.

3. That in the brown area there shall be established an international administration, the form of which is to be decided upon after consultation with Russia, and subsequently in consultation with the other Allies, and the representatives of the Shereef of Mecca.

4. That Great Britain be accorded (i) the ports of Haifa and Acre, (ii) guarantee of a given supply of water from the Tigris and Euphrates in area (A) for area (B). His Majesty's Government, on their part, undertake that they will at no time enter into negotiations for the cession of Cyprus to any third power without the previous consent of the French Government.

5. That Alexandretta shall be a free port as regards the trade of the British Empire, and that there shall be no discrimination in port charges or facilities as regards British shipping and British goods. . . .

That Haifa shall be a free port as regards the trade of France, her dominions and protectorates, and there shall be no discrimination in port charges or facilities as regards French shipping and French goods. . . .

9. It shall be agreed that the French Government will at no time enter into any negotiations for the cession of their rights and will not cede such rights in the blue area to any third Power, except the Arab State or Confederation of Arab States, without the previous agreement of His Majesty's Government who, on their part, will give a similar undertaking to the French Government regarding the red area.

(b) *Sir Edward Grey to Count Benckendorff, 23 May 1916*

. . . His Majesty's Government, on their part, in order to make the arrangement complete, are also prepared to recognize the conditions formulated by the Russian Government and accepted by the French Government in the notes exchanged at Petrograd on the 26th ultimo.

In so far, then, as these arrangements directly affect the relations of

Russia and Great Britain, I have the honour to invite the acquiescence of your Excellency's Government in an agreement on the following terms:

1. That Russia shall annex the regions of Erzeroum, Trebizond,Van, and Bitlis, up to a point subsequently to be determined on the littoral of the Black Sea to the west of Trebizond.

2. That the region of Kurdistan to the south of Van and of Bitlis between Mush, Sert, the course of the Tigris, Jezireh-ben-Omar, the crest-line of the mountains which dominate Amadia, and the region of Merga Var, shall be ceded to Russia; and that starting from the region of Merga Var, the frontier of the Arab State shall follow the crest-line of the mountains which at present divide the Ottoman and Persian Dominions. These boundaries are indicated in a general manner and are subject to modifications of detail to be proposed later by the Delimitation Commission which shall meet on the spot.

3. That the Russian Government undertake that, in all parts of the Ottoman territories thus ceded to Russia, any concessions accorded to British subjects by the Ottoman Government shall be maintained. If the Russian Government express the desire that such concessions should later be modified in order to bring them into harmony with the laws of the Russian Empire, this modification shall only take place in agreement with the British Government.

4. That in all parts of the Ottoman territories thus ceded to Russia, existing British rights of navigation and development, and the rights and privileges of any British religious, scholastic, or medical institutions shall be maintained. His Majesty's Government, on their part, undertake that similar Russian rights and privileges shall be maintained in those regions which, under the conditions of this agreement, become entirely British, or in which British rights are recognized as predominant.

B.D.F.P., 1st series, iv, 241-51

6   The Balfour Declaration, 2 November 1917

This unilateral declaration by the British Foreign Secretary addressed to the Zionist leader, Dr Weizmann, was inspired in part by a genuine idealism but contained the seeds of much future trouble. It was difficult to reconcile with the promises made to the Sherif Husein (see **XI, 4** above) and also with the Sykes-Picot agreement (see **XI, 5** above) which had envisaged some international status for Palestine. There was undoubtedly in London in 1917 a feeling that support for the Zionists could be used as a means of checking the growth of French influence in the Near East after the war.

I have much pleasure in conveying to you, on behalf of his [sic] Majesty's Government, the following declaration of sympathy with Jewish Zionist aspirations which has been submitted to and approved by the Cabinet:

His Majesty's Government view with favour the establishment in Palestine of a National Home for the Jewish People, and will use its best endeavours to facilitate the achievement of this object, it being clearly understood that nothing shall be done which may prejudice the civil and religious rights of existing non-Jewish communities in Palestine, or the rights and political status enjoyed by Jews in any other country.

A *History of the Peace Conference of Paris*, ed.
H. W. V Temperley (London, 1920-4), vi,170

7 Appeal of the Council of People's Commissars of the R.S.F.S.R. to all Muslim Workers of Russia and the East, 7 December 1917

This appeal illustrates the messianic idealism which underlay much of the foreign policy of the Bolsheviks in the aftermath of the November Revolution in Russia. The victory of Great Britain and France in November 1918 meant that this idealism was in practice directed mainly against them.

Comrades! Brothers!

Great events are occurring in Russia! An end is drawing near to the murderous war, which arose out of the bargainings of foreign powers. The rule of the plunderers, exploiting the peoples of the world, is trembling. The ancient citadel of slavery and serfdom is cracking under the blows of the Russian Revolution. The world of violence and oppression is approaching its last days. A new world is being born, a world of the toilers and the liberated. At the head of this revolution is the Workers' and Peasants' Government of Russia, the Council of People's Commissars.

Revolutionary councils of workers', soldiers', and peasants' deputies are scattered over the whole of Russia. The power in the country is in the hands of the people. The toiling masses of Russia burn with the single desire to achieve an honest peace and help the oppressed people of the world to win their freedom. . . .

The sway of capitalist plunder and violence is being undermined. The ground is slipping from under the feet of the imperialist pillagers.

In the face of these great events, we appeal to you, toiling and dispossessed Mohammedan workers, in Russia and the East. . . .

We declare that the secret treaties of the deposed Tsar regarding the annexation of Constantinople, confirmed by the late Kerensky Government, are now null and void. . . .

We declare that the treaty for the division of Turkey, which was to take Armenia from it, is null and void. . . .

Lose no time in throwing off the yoke of the ancient oppressors of your land! Let them no longer violate your hearths! You must yourselves be masters in your own land! You yourselves must arrange your life as you yourselves see fit! You have the right to do this, for your fate is in your own hands!

Comrades! Brothers!

Advance firmly and resolutely towards an honest, democratic peace!

We bear the liberation of the oppressed peoples of the world inscribed on our banners!

Mohammedans in Russia!

Mohammedans in the East!

We look to you for sympathy and support in the regeneration of the world!

> Ya. V. Klyuchnikov and A. Sabanin, *Mezh-dunarodnaya politika noveishego vremeni v dogovorakh, notakh i deklaratsiyakh* (Moscow, 1925-9), ii, 94-6

8   The Anglo-French Declaration to the Arabs, 7 November 1918

This declaration, made by the British and French governments a month after an independent state of Syria had been proclaimed by the Emir Feisal, the second son of the Sherif Husein, was regarded by Arab leaders as superseding the Sykes-Picot agreement (see **XI, 5** above); but this was not the view of the allies, and especially of the French. It thus added another element to the mass of contradictory and irreconcilable obligations with which Britain and France were burdened when peace-making began.

The object aimed at by France and Great Britain in prosecuting in the East the War let loose by the ambition of Germany is the complete and definite emancipation of the peoples so long oppressed by the Turks and the establishment of national governments and administrations deriving their authority from the initiative and free choice of the indigenous populations.

In order to carry out these intentions France and Great Britain are at one in encouraging and assisting the establishment of indigenous Governments and administrations in Syria and Mesopotamia, now liberated by the Allies, and in the territories the liberation of which they are engaged in securing, and recognizing these as soon as they are actually established.

Far from wishing to impose on the populations of these regions any particular institutions they are only concerned to ensure by their support and by adequate assistance the regular working of Governments and administrations freely chosen by the populations themselves. To secure impartial and equal justice for all, to facilitate the economic development of the country by inspiring and encouraging local initiative, to favour the diffusion of education, to put an end to dissensions that have too long been taken advantage of by Turkish policy, such is the policy which the two Allied Governments uphold in the liberated territories.

A. and P., 1938-9, xiv [Cmd 5974], pp. 50-1

9   A British View of the Position in Anatolia, June 1919

Greek forces, with British, French and American authorization, began to disembark at Smyrna on 15 May 1919, partly to forestall a possible Italian seizure of the area. The new element of bitter antagonism which this introduced into the position in Anatolia, and the stimulus it gave to the growing movement of Turkish nationalism, are described in this letter from the British Assistant High Commissioner in Turkey to a high Foreign Office official.

Admiral Webb to Sir R. Graham, 28 June 1919

What I was going to write about was the increase of friction out here between Greeks and Turks. It has now become most serious, and of course it all dates back to the time of the occupation of Smyrna by the Greek troops. This occupation has led, not unnaturally, to much bloodshed, and now it is leading to trouble everywhere in Turkey. Panderma, Broussa, Sivas, Samsoun; the story is always the same. The fact is that the Turks are getting extremely frightened, and therefore also extremely dangerous; they are concocting all sorts of wild plots, sending officers into the Interior, and generally stirring up trouble everywhere they can.

All this is really due to the indefiniteness of the situation, which gives everybody the hope that they will be altering the decision by creating a 'fait accompli', the Greeks by occupying places in the Interior, ostensibly on the plea of lack of public security, and the Turks by organizing defensive measures to impress upon Europe the strength of National feeling.

We have just been concocting a telegram to you on the subject for Admiral Calthorpe's[1] approval, to try and make it clear that (? the time for) local expedients is past. Up to the time of the Smyrna landing we were getting on quite well. The Turk was, of course, somewhat troublesome, but we were gradually getting the bad Valis, Mutessarifs, etc., removed, and I think we could have got along very well without any big trouble until the Peace. It was just a matter of sitting tight, and getting the Turkish Government to do what we wanted. But now things are quite changed. Greeks and Turks are killing one another wholesale in the Aidin Vilayet. Moustapha Kemal is busy round Samsoun, and so far refuses to come to heel. Raouf Bey and one or two others are getting very busy down Panderma way, and there are symptoms which seem to point to the Ministry of War here at Constantinople being the organizing centre of the disturbances.

There is a point which very closely affects our prestige, and our often expressed desire for the avoidance of bloodshed. Both parties to the quarrel – both Greeks and Turks – are fully aware that when the Smyrna decision was arrived at, and communicated by us to the Turkish Government, we were throwing an apple of discord down between the two parties. The discord has taken place, and has led to much bloodshed. Both sides now look to the Entente as a whole, but to us in particular, to clear up the mess, to define the situation, and to have it confirmed, not by orders which may arrive from day to day, but by the printed text of the Treaty of Peace.

You will readily realize that our reiterated advice to both parties to live in amity and affection is considered somewhat hypocritical when we do our best to create a situation which sets them at each other's throats in the present, and lays up the seeds of hostility indefinitely in the future.

Quite apart from anything else, the economical effects resulting from this situation are disastrous to a country which has been brought up to the verge of financial and economic ruin, and I venture to think that

[1] The British naval Commander-in-Chief in the Mediterranean.

we are hopelessly prejudicing the future chances of recuperation for thousands of Christians, whose welfare we have so much at heart, and concerning which we have made so many protestations.

I cannot press this point too strongly, for it may quite possibly result in this country having to be fed from the outside next winter, instead of feeding others, as it might have done, to the benefit of its exhausted exchequer.

All these considerations can only lead up to one conclusion, and that is the essential need for giving Turkey *a very early peace*. I hope and believe that the peace terms will be severe and drastic, but let us have them quickly. Every day makes the situation more difficult and dangerous, and every day adds to the degree of hate, now extremely intense, which exists in this country between Moslems and Christians.

B D.F.P., 1st series, iv, 655–6

10   An American View of the Position in Syria and Palestine, July 1919

The authors of this report headed an American commission of enquiry (the King-Crane Commission) sent by President Wilson in the summer of 1919 to investigate the wishes of the peoples of Syria and Palestine with regard to the allocation by the newly-founded League of Nations of mandates over them. It can be regarded as the most impartial contemporary statement of the position in this respect.

C. R. Crane and H. C. King to the Commission to Negotiate Peace, Beirut, 10 July 1919 (telegram)

ommission has now covered strategic points from Beersheba to Baalbek and from Mediterranean Sea to Amman. Every facility has been given Commission by various military governors, though inevitable some steering. Heartily welcomed everywhere. No doubt of great interest of people, some Bedouin delegates riding 30 hours to meet Commission. Gratitude to you and Americans constantly and warmly expressed. Popular program developing in range and definiteness showing considerable political insight. Much to indicate our enquiries greatly worthwhile and freer expression of opinion to American section than could have been made to mixed commission. Certain points are unmistakable. Intense desire for unity of all Syria and Palestine and for as early independence as possible. Unexpectedly strong expressions of national feeling. Singularly determined repulsion to becoming a mere colony of any power and against any kind of French mandate. Only marked exceptions to this statement are found in strong parties of Lebanese who demand complete separation of Lebanon with French collaboration. In our judgement proclamation of French mandate for all Syria would precipitate warfare between Arabs and French, and force Great Britain to dangerous alternative. America generally first choice of most for mandatory because believed have no territorial ambition. General demand that essentially, same condition should hold for Iraq as for Syria. Both British Government and French officers share conviction that unity of whole of Syria and Palestine is most desirable. They feel that constant friction and danger to peace are otherwise inevitable between British subjects, French and Arabs. But there is little clear evidence that either British Government or French Government are willing entirely to withdraw. Subsequent experience only confirms earlier dispatch [sic] concerning Zionism. Syria National Congress composed of 69 regularly elected representatives Moslems and Christians from Syria including Palestine and Lebanon met at Damascus July 2nd. Formulated program acceptable to all Moslems and many Christians, except that Christians preferring strong mandatory power for their protection. Congress asks immediate complete political independence for united Syria. Government a civil, constitutionalist, federal monarchy, safely guarding right of minority under Prince Feisal as king. Affirm Article 22 of Covenant does not apply to Syria. Mandate interpreted to mean economy [sic] and technical assistance limited in time. Asking this earnestly from America. Should America refuse then England. Deny all rights and refuse all assistance of France. Vigorously oppose Zionistic plan and Jewish immigration. Asking complete independence of Mesopotamia. Protesting against Sykes-Picot Agreement and Balfour Declaration. Concluding request that political rights be not less than under Turkey. . . .

[Ends by stressing importance of the Syria-Palestine problem and strongly recommending support for King Feisal].

Papers Relating to the Foreign Relations of the
United States: The Paris Peace Conference, 1919,
xii (Washington, 1947), 749-50

II   The Treaty of Sèvres, 10 August 1920

The peace treaty with Turkey of which the most important political clauses are given below was extremely severe, since it not only took from the Ottoman

Empire all its former Arab possessions but also deprived the Turkish government of control of the Straits, envisaged at least temporary Greek control of the Smyrna area, and created an independent Armenian state. But the allies, partly because of other preoccupations and partly because of hopes that the United States might accept a mandate for Armenia or the Straits area, had delayed too long in making peace. The rise of Turkish nationalism was to make it impossible to enforce the treaty.

PART III. POLITICAL CLAUSES

Section I. Constantinople

Article 36. Subject to the provisions of the present Treaty, the High Contracting Parties agree that the rights and title of the Turkish Government over Constantinople shall not be affected, and that the said Government and His Majesty the Sultan shall be entitled to reside there and to maintain there the capital of the Turkish State.

Nevertheless, in the event of Turkey failing to observe faithfully the provisions of the present Treaty, or of any treaties or conventions supplementary thereto, particularly as regards the protection of the rights of racial, religious or linguistic minorities, the Allied Powers expressly reserve the right to modify the above provisions, and Turkey hereby agrees to accept any dispositions which may be taken in this connection.

Section II. Straits

Article 37. The navigation of the Straits, including the Dardanelles, the Sea of Marmora and the Bosphorus, shall in future be open, both in peace and war, to every vessel of commerce or of war and to military and commercial aircraft, without distinction of flag.

These waters shall not be subject to blockade, nor shall any belligerent right be exercised nor any act of hostility be committed within them, unless in pursuance of a decision of the Council of the League of Nations.

Article 38. The Turkish Government recognizes that it is necessary to take further measures to ensure the freedom of navigation provided for in Article 37, and accordingly delegates, so far as it is concerned, to a Commission to be called the 'Commission of the Straits', and hereinafter referred to as 'the Commission', the control of the waters specified in Article 39.

Article 39. The authority of the Commission will extend to all the water between the Mediterranean mouth of the Dardanelles and the Black

Sea mouth of the Bosphorus, and to the waters within three miles of each of these mouths.

This authority may be exercised on shore to such extent as may be necessary for the execution of the provisions of this Section.

Section IV. Smyrna . . .

Article 69. The city of Smyrna and the territory defined in Article 66 remain under Turkish sovereignty. Turkey however transfers to the Greek Government the exercise of her rights of sovereignty over the city of Smyrna and the said territory. In witness of such sovereignty the Turkish flag shall remain permanently hoisted over an outer fort in the town of Smyrna. The fort will be designated by the Principal Allied Powers.

Article 70. The Greek Government will be responsible for the administration of the city of Smyrna and the territory defined in Article 66, and will effect this administration by means of a body of officials which it will appoint specially for the purpose.

Article 71. The Greek Government shall be entitled to maintain in the city of Smyrna and the territory defined in Article 66 the military forces required for the maintenance of order and public security.

Article 72. A local parliament shall be set up with an electoral system calculated to ensure proportional representation of all sections of the population, including racial, linguistic and religious minorities. . . .

Article 83. When a period of five years shall have elapsed after the coming into force of the present Treaty the local parliament referred to in Article 72 may, by a majority of votes, ask the Council of the League of Nations for the definitive incorporation in the Kingdom of Greece of the city of Smyrna and the territory defined in Article 66. The Council may require, as a preliminary, a plebiscite under conditions which it will lay down.

In the event of such incorporation as a result of the application of the foregoing paragraph, the Turkish sovereignty referred to in Article 69 shall cease. Turkey hereby renounces in that event in favour of Greece all rights and title over the city of Smyrna and the territory defined in Article 66.

Section VI. Armenia

Article 88. Turkey, in accordance with the action already taken by the

Allied Powers, hereby recognises Armenia as a free and independent State.

A. and P., 1920, li [Cmd.964], pp. 16-25

12   The Turkish National Pact, 28 January 1920

This declaration (approved by the newly-elected Turkish Parliament in Constantinople on 28 January 1920, but drawn up earlier in Ankara, the head-quarters of the nationalists) shows how Turkish national feeling, led by Musta-pha Kemal, was now reacting to allied pressure and above all to the Greek threat in Anatolia. Its terms, which largely repeated a nationalist declaration issued at Sivas on 9 September 1919, were incompatible with the creation of an Armenian state, the Greek occupation of part of Asia Minor, or (Article VI) with the continuance of the economic and legal privileges enjoyed for cen-turies by many foreigners under the system of Capitulations.

The Members of the Ottoman Chamber of Deputies recognise and affirm that the independence of the State and the future of the Nation can be assured by complete respect for the following principles, which represent the maximum of sacrifice which can be undertaken in order to achieve a just and lasting peace, and that the continued existence of a stable Ottoman Sultanate and society is impossible outside of the said principles:

Article I. Inasmuch as it is necessary that the destinies of the portions of the Turkish Empire which are populated exclusively by an Arab majority, and which on the conclusion of the armistice of 30th October 1918 were in the occupation of enemy forces, should be determined in accordance with the votes which shall be freely given by the inhabi-tants, the whole of those parts whether within or outside the said armistice line which are inhabited by an Ottoman Moslem majority, united in religion, in race and in aim, imbued with sentiments of mutual respect for each other and of sacrifice, and wholly respectful of each other's racial and social rights and surrounding conditions, form a whole which does not admit of division for any reason in truth or in ordinance.

Article II. We accept that, in the case of the three Sandjaks which united themselves by a general vote to the mother country when they first were free, recourse should again be had, if necessary, to a free popular vote.

Article III. The determination of the juridical status of Western Thrace also, which has been made dependent on the Turkish peace, must be effected in accordance with the votes which shall be given by the inhabitants in complete freedom.

Article IV. The security of the city of Constantinople, which is the seat of the Caliphate of Islam, the capital of the Sultanate, and the headquarters of the Ottoman Government, and of the Sea of Marmora, must be protected from every danger. Provided this principle is maintained, whatever decision may be arrived at jointly by us and all other Governments concerned, regarding the opening of the Bosphorus to the commerce and traffic of the world, is valid.

Article V. The rights of minorities as defined in the treaties concluded between the Entente Powers and their enemies and certain of their associates shall be confirmed and assured by us – in reliance on the belief that the Moslem minorities in neighbouring countries also will have the benefit of the same rights.

Article VI. It is a fundamental condition of our life and continued existence that we, like every country, should enjoy complete independence and liberty in the matter of assuring the means of our development, in order that our national and economic development should be rendered possible and that it should be possible to conduct affairs in the form of a more up-to-date regular administration.

For this reason we are opposed to restrictions inimical to our development in political, judicial, financial, and other matters.

The conditions of settlement of our proved debts shall likewise not be contrary to these principles.

> A. J. Toynbee, *The Western Question in Greece and Turkey* (London, 1922), pp. 209-10

13 Russo-Turkish Treaty of Friendship, 16 March 1921

Ideologically the nationalism of Mustapha Kemal and his followers had nothing in common with the Marxism of the Bolsheviks. However the two groups were throughout most of 1920 being brought together by common fear of the Western Powers, above all Great Britain, and common hostility to the Treaty of Sèvres. This treaty marks the culmination of the forced rapprochement between them. Note in particular Article V which, if put into practice, would exclude from the Straits and the Black Sea the western naval influence which both parties feared and disliked.

The Government of the Russian Socialist Federal Soviet Republic and the Government of the Grand National Assembly of Turkey, sharing as they do the principles of the brotherhood of nations and the right of each nation to determine its own fate, and taking into consideration, moreover, the solidarity between them in the struggle against imperialism, foreseeing that any difficulties created for the one would render worse the position of the other, and inspired by the desire to bring about lasting good relations and uninterrupted sincere friendship between themselves, based on mutual interests, have decided to sign an agreement of friendship and brotherhood. . . .

Article I. Each of the contracting parties agrees in principle not to recognize any peace treaty or other international agreement which has been imposed upon the other by force. The Government of the R.S.F.S.R. agrees not to recognize any international agreement relating to Turkey which is not recognized by the National Government of Turkey, at present represented by the Grand National Assembly.

The expression 'Turkey' in the present treaty is understood to mean the territories included in the Turkish National Pact on the 28th January, 1920, elaborated and proclaimed by the Ottoman Chamber of Deputies in Constantinople, and communicated to the press and to all oreign Governments. . . .

Article II. Turkey agrees to cede to Georgia the right of suzerainty over the town and port of Batum and the territory situated to the north of the frontier mentioned in Article I, forming a part of the district of Batum, on the following conditions [its population to have 'a generous measure of autonomy' and Turkey to have free transit for imports and exports through the port without payment of customs duties]. . . .

Article IV. The contracting parties, establishing contact between the national movement for the liberation of the Eastern peoples and the struggle of the workers of Russia for a new social order, solemnly recognize the right of these nations to freedom and independence, and in the same way their right to choose a form of government according o their own wishes.

Article V. In order to assure the opening of the Straits and the free passage of merchant ships of all nations, the contracting parties agree to entrust the final elaboration of an international régime of the Black

Sea and the Straits to a future conference composed of delegates of the littoral States, on condition that the decisions of the above-mentioned conference shall not inflict damage on the full sovereignty of Turkey or on the security of Turkey or of Constantinople, her capital. . . .

Article XIV. The contracting parties agree to conclude in the near future a consular convention and other arrangements regulating all economic, financial and other questions which are necessary for the establishment of friendly relations between the two countries, as set forth in the preamble to the present treaty.

Dokumenty Vneshnei Politiki SSSR, iii
(Moscow, 1959), 597-601

14   The Treaty of Lausanne, 24 July 1923

By this treaty, which can be regarded as marking the end of the Eastern Question in the form which it had taken for the last century and a half, Turkey lost all her Arab possessions as well as the Dodecanese islands (which had been in Italian occupation since 1911). In Europe she was left with only eastern Thrace. However she recovered the whole of Anatolia, as well as the islands most needed for the defence of the Dardanelles, and was now for the first time in her history a largely national state. She was also able to avoid the payment of any war indemnity (the only defeated power in the First World War to do so) and to end completely the hated régime of capitulations (the issue on which the negotiations were most prolonged and difficult). The complex Straits Convention annexed to the treaty, of which the main points are given here, was superseded by the Montreux Convention of 1936.

. . . .

Article 2. [Defines the European frontier of Turkey from the Black Sea o the Aegean.]

Article 3. [Defines the Asiatic frontier of Turkey, from the Mediterranean to the frontier of Persia.] . . .

Article 12. The decision taken on the 13th February, 1914, by the Conference of London, in virtue of Articles 5 of the Treaty of London of the 30th May, 1913, and 15 of the Treaty of Athens of the 14th November, 1913, which decision was communicated to the Greek Government on the 13th February, 1914, regarding the sovereignty of Greece over the islands of the Eastern Mediterranean, other than the islands of Imbros, Samothrace, Mytilene, Chios, Samos and Nikaria, is confirmed, subject to the provisions of the present Treaty respecting the islands placed under the sovereignty of Italy, which form the subject of Article 15. . . .

Article 15. Turkey renounces in favour of Italy all rights and title over the following islands: Stampalia, Rhodes, Calki, Scarpanto, Casos, Piscopis, Misiros, Calimnos, Leros, Patmos, Lipsos, Simi and Cos, which are now occupied by Italy, and the islets dependent thereon, and also over the island of Castellorizzo . . ..

Article 17. The renunciation by Turkey of all rights and titles over Egypt and over the Soudan will take effect as from the 5th November, 1914. . . .

Article 20. Turkey hereby recognizes the annexation of Cyprus proclaimed by the British Government on the 5th November, 1914. . . .

Article 28. Each of the High Contracting Parties hereby accepts, in so far as it is concerned, the complete abolition of the Capitulations in Turkey in every respect. . . .

Article 38. The Turkish Government undertakes to assure full and complete protection of life and liberty to all inhabitants of Turkey without distinction of birth, nationality, language, race or religion.

All inhabitants of Turkey shall be entitled to free exercise, whether in public or private, of any creed, religion or belief, the observance of which shall not be incompatible with public order and good morals.

Non-Moslem minorities will enjoy full freedom of movement and of emigration, subject to the measures applied, on the whole or on part of the territory, to all Turkish nationals, and which may be taken by the Turkish Government for national defence, or for the maintenance of public order.

Article 39. Turkish nationals belonging to non-Moslem minorities will enjoy the same civil and political rights as Moslems.

All the inhabitants of Turkey, without distinction of religion, shall be equal before the law. . . .

Article 58. Turkey, on the one hand, and the other Contracting Powers (except Greece) on the other hand, reciprocally renounce all pecuniary claims for the loss and damage suffered respectively by Turkey and the said Powers and by their nationals . . . between the 1st August, 1914, and the coming into force of the present Treaty as the result of acts of war, or measures of requisition, sequestration, disposal or confiscation.

Convention relating to the Régime of the Straits

Article 1. The High Contracting Parties agree to recognise and declare the principle of freedom of transit and of navigation by sea and by air in the Strait of the Dardanelles, the Sea of Marmora and the Bosphorus, hereinafter comprised under the general term of the 'Straits'.

Article 2. The transit and navigation of commercial vessels and aircraft, and of war vessels and aircraft in the Straits in time of peace and in time of war shall henceforth be regulated by the provisions of the attached annex.

ANNEX

Rules for the Passage of Commercial Vessels and Aircraft, and of War Vessels and Aircraft through the Straits

.   .   .   .

Article 2. Warships, including Fleet Auxiliaries, Troopships, Aircraft Carriers and Military Aircraft

a) *In Time of Peace.* Complete freedom of passage by day and by night under any flag, without any formalities, or tax, or charge whatever, but subject to the following restrictions as to the total force:

The maximum force which any one Power may send through the Straits into the Black Sea is not to be greater than that of the most powerful fleet of the littoral Powers of the Black Sea existing in that sea at the time of passage; but with the proviso that the Powers reserve to themselves the right to send into the Black Sea, at all times and under all circumstances, a force of not more than three ships of which no individual ship shall exceed 10,000 tons.

Turkey has no responsibility in regard to the number of war vessels which pass through the Straits. . . .

b) *In Time of War, Turkey being Neutral.* Complete freedom of passage by day and by night under any flag, without any formalities, or tax, or charge whatever, under the same limitations as in paragraph 2 a). . . .

c) *In Time of War, Turkey being Belligerent.* Complete freedom of passage for neutral warships, without any formalities, or tax, or charge whatever, but under the same limitations as in paragraph 2 a).

The measures taken by Turkey to prevent enemy ships and aircraft from using the Straits are not to be of such a nature as to prevent the free passage of neutral ships and aircraft, and Turkey agrees to provide the said ships and aircraft with either the necessary instructions or pilots for the above purpose. . . .

Article 4. The zones and islands indicated below shall be demilitarized:
a) Both shores of the Straits of the Dardanelles and the Bosphorus over the extent of the zones delimited below. . . . [Goes on to give details of these.]
b) All the islands in the Sea of Marmora, with the exception of the island of Emir Ali Adasi.
c) In the Aegean Sea, the islands of Samothrace, Lemnos, Imbros, Tenedos and Rabbit Islands. . . .

Article 8. At Constantinople, including for this purpose Stamboul, Pera, Galata, Scutari, as well as Princes' Islands, and in the immediate neighbourhood of Constantinople, there may be maintained for the requirements of the capital, a garrison with a maximum strength of 12,000 men. An arsenal and naval base may also be maintained at Constantinople. . . .

Article 10. There shall be constituted at Constantinople an International Commission composed in accordance with Article 12 and called the 'Straits Commission'. . . .

Article 12. The Commission shall be composed of a representative of Turkey, who shall be President, and representatives of France, Great Britain, Italy, Japan, Bulgaria, Greece, Roumania, Russia, and the Serb-Croat-Slovene State, in so far as these Powers are signatories of the present Convention, each of these Powers being entitled to representation as from its ratification of the said Convention. . . .

Article 14. It will be the duty of the Commission to see that the provisions relating to the passage of warships and military aircraft are carried out; these provisions are laid down in paragraphs 2, 3 and 4 of the Annex to Article 2.

A. and P., 1923, xxv [Cmd.1929], pp. 13-31, 49, 113-25

GLOSSARY

The terms listed are given in the forms used in the documents where they are quoted. The generally accepted modern form, where it differs, is given in brackets.

BOSTANGIS (BOSTANCIS): Lit. 'gardeners'; a military corps so called because it was first formed to cultivate the ground around the Sultan's palace. In addition to its military functions it also performed a variety of police and other duties in connection with the palace.

CAPUDAN (KAPUDAN) PASHA: Commander of the Turkish fleet.

CORBACI: Commander of an *orta* of Janissaries.

ETMEIDAN (OKMAIDAN): Lit. 'archery ground'; a large open space above the Arsenal in Constantinople.

FADA'I: Lit. 'he who offers up his life', a term originally used of the Ismaili sect in the Middle Ages; hence one who sacrifices himself for national or patriotic purposes.

HATT-I SHERIF: Decree of the Sultan.

IMAM: Religious leader; basically the man who indicated the ritual movements to the congregation during a Muslim service.

JANISSARIES: A powerful and privileged military corps, originally recruited, from the early fifteen century onwards, by a levy of children from the Christian population of the Ottoman Empire. From the later sixteenth century, as they degenerated into a vested interest, they were the most important force opposing reform of the empire.

CAIMACAN (KAIMAKAM): Lit. 'deputy'; originally a Vizir who replaced at Constantinople the Grand Vizir when the latter was on campaign.

MAMELUKES (MAMLUKS): The ruling group in Egypt until the early nineteenth century; recruited largely from Georgian and Circassian slaves and distinguished by selfishness and factionalism.

MUFTI: An authority on Islamic law: the Mufti of Constantinople was the highest religious dignitary in the Ottoman Empire.

MUTESSARIF: Provincial governor, governor of a *Sandjak*.

ORDA (ORTA): A Janissary regiment.

QADI (KADI): Judge administering Islamic religious and customary law.

RAMAZAN (RAMADAN): The ninth month of the Muslim calendar, during which the faithful fast during the day. In the eighteenth and nineteenth centuries trade and industry were largely at a standstill during this period.

RAYA: Peasants not members of the Muslim ruling structure of the Ottoman Empire; in the eighteenth and nineteenth centuries the term is applied particularly to the Christian population of the Empire.

SEYMANS (SEĞMENS): One of the three divisions which made up the Janissary corps.

SERASKIER: War Minister.

THALWEG: The mid-channel of a river; the line along which the valley in which the river runs is deepest.

TOPCI (TOPÇU): A gunner, member of the corps of gunners created in the Ottoman army early in the fifteenth century.

ULEMA: Those learned in Islamic religious law and tradition: the nearest Islamic equivalent to a priestly class.

YENITCHERY AGHASSI (YENIÇERI AGASI): Aga (commander) of the Janissaries.

SHORT LIST OF BOOKS FOR
FURTHER READING

Anderson, M. S., *The Eastern Question, 1774-1923: A Study in International Relations* (1966).

Crawley, C. W., *The Question of Greek Independence, 1821-1833* (1930).

Ghorbal, S., *The Beginnings of the Egyptian Question and the Rise of Mehemet Ali* (1928).

Hoskins, H. L., *British Routes to India* (1928).

Howard, H. N., *The Partition of Turkey: A Diplomatic History, 1913-1923* (1931).

Hurewitz, J. C., *Diplomacy in the Near and Middle East: A Documentary Record* (1956).

Kedourie, E., *England and the Middle East: The Destruction of the Ottoman Empire, 1914-1921* (1956).

Lewis, B., *The Emergence of Modern Turkey* (London, 1961).

Medlicott, W. N., *The Congress of Berlin and After* (1938).

Mosse, W. E., *The Rise and Fall of the Crimean System, 1855-1871* (London, 1963).

Puryear, V. J., *Napoleon and the Dardanelles* (1951).

Robinson, R., and Gallagher, J., *Africa and the Victorians* (1961).

Schmitt, B., *The Annexation of Bosnia* (1937).

Sumner, B. H., *Russia and the Balkans, 1870-1880* (1937).

Temperley, H. W. V., *England and the Near East: The Crimea* (1936).

Wolf, J., *The Diplomatic History of the Baghdad Railroad* (1936).